A NIGHT ON THE TILES

by Frank Vickery

I0154506

SAMUEL FRENCH

written permission of the publisher. No one shall share this title, or part of this title, to any social media or file hosting websites.

The moral right of Frank Vickery to be identified as author of this work has been asserted in accordance with Section 77 of the Copyright, Designs and Patents Act 1988.

USE OF COPYRIGHTED MUSIC

A licence issued by Concord Theatricals to perform this play does not include permission to use the incidental music specified in this publication. In the United Kingdom: Where the place of performance is already licensed by the PERFORMING RIGHT SOCIETY (PRS) a return of the music used must be made to them. If the place of performance is not so licensed then application should be made to PRS for Music (www.prsformusic.com). A separate and additional licence from PHONOGRAPHIC PERFORMANCE LTD (www.ppluk.com) may be needed whenever commercial recordings are used. Outside the United Kingdom: Please contact the appropriate music licensing authority in your territory for the rights to any incidental music.

USE OF COPYRIGHTED THIRD-PARTY MATERIALS

Licensees are solely responsible for obtaining formal written permission from copyright owners to use copyrighted third-party materials (e.g., artworks, logos) in the performance of this play and are strongly cautioned to do so. If no such permission is obtained by the licensee, then the licensee must use only original materials that the licensee owns and controls. Licensees are solely responsible and liable for clearances of all third-party copyrighted materials, and shall indemnify the copyright owners of the play(s) and their licensing agent, Concord Theatricals Ltd., against any costs, expenses, losses and liabilities arising from the use of such copyrighted third-party materials by licensees.

IMPORTANT BILLING AND CREDIT REQUIREMENTS

If you have obtained performance rights to this title, please refer to your licensing agreement for important billing and credit requirements.

A NIGHT ON THE TILES

Performed at the Parc and Dare Theatre, Treorchy, in May 1986 by the Parc and Dare Theatre Company and subsequently at the Duke of York's Theatre, London on 10th August 1986 with the following cast of characters:

Doris	Lynfa Williams
Reg	Kelvin Lawrence-Jones
Kenneth	Frank Vickery
Gareth	Huw Thomas
Grandad	Brian Meadows
Mrs Morris	Iris Griffiths
Shirley	Lorraine John

Directed by Brian Meadows

The play's first professional performance was at the Coliseum Theatre, Oldham, on 22nd January, 1987, with the following cast of characters:

Doris	Veronica Doran
Reg	Steve Halliwell
Kenneth	Malcolm Skates
Gareth	David Birrell
Grandad	William Maxwell
Mrs Morris	Paula Tilbrook
Shirley	Meriel Schofield

Directed by John Retallack

SYNOPSIS OF SCENES

The action of the play takes place in the back yard or garden of the family's terraced house

ACT I
  SCENE 1   9.30 am on a bright and sunny morning in
            early May
  SCENE 2   10.30 pm the same night.

ACT II
  SCENE 1   12.00 midday in a very hot August
  SCENE 2   Later the same afternoon

ACT III
  SCENE 1   7.45 pm on a warm late September night
  SCENE 2   About 10.00 pm the same evening

Time—the present

You will also enjoy other plays by Frank Vickery including:

After I'm Gone (1 act)
A Night Out (1 act)
One O'Clock From The House (3 acts)

Titles to come:

All's Fair
Family Planning

ACT I

SCENE 1

The back yard or garden of a terraced house. It is 9.30 am on a bright and sunny morning in early May

When the CURTAIN *rises, the sun is shining brightly and the birds are singing. There is no-one on stage. Inside the house from the small kitchen a radio can be heard. Just as this tranquil morning is being presented to us, Doris is heard calling from the kitchen to Gareth, who is asleep upstairs*

Doris (*off, screaming*) Gareth! Gareth. Come on, get up, I'm not calling you again—it's half-past nine.

The radio is turned up

Reg (*off*) Turn, that bloody thing down, you'll wake the dead.
Doris (*off*) Wake the dead? (*She turns the radio down*) I'll be grateful if it just gets him up of bed. He's not a bit concerned—not a bit. Four times I've called him this morning—four times and he's still not up. You wouldn't think he was getting married this morning. Where's my father?
Reg (*off*) Out the toilet.

The back door opens and Doris stands half out

Doris Dad, your breakfast is on the table.
Grandad (*from inside the loo*) Righto!

Doris goes back into the house

Doris (*off*) It's not fair. When does he think I'm going to have time to get myself ready? I've been up since six o'clock and all I've done is iron shirts and cook breakfast—and there's him up there just can't be bothered ... (*Screaming again*) Gareth—it's quarter-past ten.

Reg (*off*) That's the quickest three-quarters of an hour I've ever spent.
Doris (*off*) Well I've got to tell him something, haven't I, or I'll never get him up.
Reg (*off*) Try taking him up a cup of tea.
Doris (*off*) I warned him. I told him last week not to have his bachelor party on the Friday before. Well I mean it's asking for trouble—it's asking for it. I bet he'll look a sight, judging by the way he came in last night. It's Kenneth that put him up to that though.
Reg (*off*) Put him up to what?
Doris (*off*) To having his party the night before. He'll do anything for

devilment that boy. I know him of old. He knows our Gareth can't drink so he probably did it just to see him in a state. It's all right for him though.
Reg (*off*) For who?
Doris (*off*) For Kenneth. He's like you. Put anything in front of you and as long as it's wet you'll drink it. Where is he anyway?
Reg (*off*) Who?
Doris (*off*) Kenneth.
Reg (*off*) In the shower.
Doris (*off, screaming*) Kenneth!

Kenneth enters the kitchen

Kenneth (*standing behind her*) I'm here. (*He frightens her*)

Plates are heard crashing to the floor

Doris (*off, shouting at the top of her voice*) Don't stand behind me like that you frightened the life out of me. And look at that bacon. Pick it up, quick before the dog gets it.
Kenneth (*off*) I'm not eating it now.
Doris (*off*) Well it's not going to get wasted—not at one pound fifty a pound it's not. Put it on Grandad's plate—he won't know any difference. Now get out of my way before you do any more damage.
Kenneth (*off*) That's right—put the blame on me.
Reg (*off*) Have you finished in the shower, Ken?
Kenneth (*off*) Yes Dad.
Doris (*off*) Don't sit down there, Kenneth.
Kenneth (*off*) Why?
Doris (*off*) Because I'll want that chair to stand on now in a minute. Out of my way, I've got boiling water in this kettle, and don't stand in front of the fire, I'm airing your grandfather's shirt.

The back door opens and Kenneth comes out into the garden. He stretches and looks up to the sky. He takes a few deep breaths and strolls over to the loo. He tries to open the door

Grandad (*from inside*) I'm in here.

Kenneth walks along the path then on to the small green. He begins to do press-ups on the grass, but after he has completed about three he collapses. He just lies there exhausted

Doris comes to the back door and calls again

Doris Dad, this bacon's getting cold.
Grandad (*from the loo*) All right I'll be there now.

Doris goes back into the house

Kenneth rolls over on to his back and calls to Grandad—mimicking his mother

Kenneth It's getting cold, Dad and I'm not calling you again.
Grandad (*from the loo*) I'll be there now I said.

Doris comes to the back door again

Doris What's that Dad? (*Calling*) Dad!
Grandad (*from the loo*) What?
Doris I thought you said something.
Grandad (*from the loo*) I thought you called me.
Doris Don't be long.

Doris goes back indoors

Kenneth (*in his mother's voice*) Dad?
Grandad (*from the loo*) What?
Kenneth (*in his grandfather's voice*) Doris?

Doris appears, screaming at the back door

Doris What!
Grandad (*shouting from inside the loo*) What!
Doris What do you want?
Grandad Nothing!
Doris Well hurry up then!

She goes inside

Kenneth has hysterics on the green

(*Off, calling*) I'm pouring the—good God almighty—you're down. Have you seen what you look like? There's a tube of Alka-Seltzer in the cupboard, take them—take them all. You look like last Sunday's cabbage. Cup of tea? What's the matter, can't you speak? I'm not surprised either. You wouldn't listen to your mother though, would you? Wouldn't have it that she knew best. Not that I blame you really. It's that idiot you've got for a brother. It's him I should be laying it into not you.

At this point Gareth comes into the garden. He is still in his pyjamas. His hair is in a mess, in fact he looks a complete wreck. Having left the house he stands dazed for a few moments before making for the loo

But he can do no wrong in your eye though, can he? Shield him to the last you will, won't you? Laughing at you that's all he was doing—laughing at you. But of course you can't see that. You don't want to see it. You don't like to think that ... well where the hell has he gone now? (*Calling*) Gareth?

He doesn't answer

Gareth!

He is at the toilet door

/ Gareth!

Gareth tries opening the door

Grandad (*from inside*) I'm in here.
Kenneth (*still flat out on the grass*) Oh you're up then, are you?

Gareth turns round and sees him

Hey, don't let on to the old girl but I think he's been there since last night. (*He gets up and sits on the bench*) You wouldn't remember much about last night though, would you?

Gareth shakes his head. He moves in the direction of the bench

Did you enjoy it?

Gareth nods

What's the matter, can't you speak?

He shakes his head

Come on, try. You'll be great once you've got the first word out. Say, greasy sausage and runny eggs.

Gareth is about to throw up

No—all right, then. Your name, then. My name. Anything. Come on.

Gareth tries with all his might but all he eventually manages is a pathetic groan. They both find this funny

Well, that's a start anyway. Try again, come on. Ga ... Ga ... Gareth.¹ Gareth ... come on.

Gareth this time does manage something that does vaguely resemble his name

That's it. It's coming. Now say it again.

Gareth says his name three or four times and by the end of it he is saying his name quite clearly

There you are. You're away now.

Gareth shouts his name rather loudly. Then grimaces with pain

Don't get carried away.

Gareth (*still speaking with difficulty*) I don't think I've got a roof to my mouth.

Kenneth You're lucky you've still got a top to your head. You put me and everyone else in the shade last night.

Gareth Why, what did I do?

Kenneth What did you do? You only drank everything in sight, that's all. (*Getting up and moving* R) Still, not to worry. I mean only once in your life you have a stag night, don't you? Unless you're lucky, of course, and get married twice.

Gareth Unless you're luckier still and don't get married at all.

Kenneth What's the matter with you? You haven't got cold feet, have you?

Gareth Are you kidding? I've got to go through with it now or the old girl will kill me.

Kenneth Shirley?

Gareth No, (*nodding towards the house*) that old girl.

Kenneth Oh, I don't know what you're worrying about her for. I mean it's not her you're marrying, is it?

Gareth No, I know. Thank God. I'd hate to think Shirley would turn out like that.

Kenneth (*moving to sit on the arm of the bench, next to Gareth's left*) I reckon he deserves a medal, you know. Our dad ought to be awarded the George Cross or something like that. He deserves it after living with our mam for twenty-five years.

Gareth Twenty-six.

Kenneth That's what they've told us, but twenty-five it is.

Gareth It can't be, you're twenty-five.

Kenneth (*looking at Gareth and smiling*) I rest my case.

Gareth Get out of it. (*He smiles and thinks about it*) Honest?

Kenneth Yeah. So you see, you and Shirley are just keeping up the family tradition.

Gareth I wondered why she didn't fly off the handle when I told her. (*After a slight pause*) It's a bit hard to imagine though, isn't it? Her and Dad like— you know, (*he makes a fist and bends his arm at the elbow*) before they were married.

Kenneth It didn't surprise me. (*Moving down* L) She looked a right little raver in her wedding photos. Didn't you think so? Well it was either that or she fancied the photographer. Anything with a zoom lens. Get it?

The toilet flushes

There's hopes.

Gareth And you've seen the licence?

Kenneth (*nodding*) It's upstairs in that square biscuit tin on top of the wardrobe. I'll show it to you next time I get a chance. (*He begins to sing*) "I'm getting married in the morning. Ding dong . . ." (*He takes Gareth's head in his hands and rocks it to and fro*)

Gareth almost vomits

". . . the bells are going to chime."

Grandad is having trouble opening the toilet door. After a few attempts he resorts to calling for help

Grandad (*from the loo*) Doris. Doris, the door is stuck again. (*Calling louder*) Doris.

Kenneth (*crossing to the loo*) I'd better bale him out. ,

Grandad Can you do it, Doris?

Kenneth It's me, Grandad.

Grandad Oh, Gareth, is it?

Kenneth No. Ken.

Grandad I can't get out, Ken.

Kenneth I know, Grandad. I'll open it now, in a minute. (*He struggles with the latch*) I can't seem to shift it.

Gareth comes across to help Ken but the door still won't open

Pull the handle towards you, Grandad?

Grandad Pull the handle?

Kenneth Yes, that's right.

Still nothing happens

It's no good. (*Calling to the house*) Mam? (*After a pause*) Mam?

Doris comes to the back door

Doris What's the matter now?

Kenneth It's Grandad. He's locked in the khazi.

Doris (*drying her wet hands on her overall*) Again? He's forever doing it. Out of my way. (*Doris forces herself between them*) Dad? Move your feet. Sit sideways on the pan. (*To Kenneth*) We wouldn't have this trouble if he opened the door standing up.

Grandad Sit sideways?

Doris That's right. (*She presses the latch and the door opens*) There we are.

Grandad comes out, wearing his underclothes. He is holding the inside part of the handle in his hand

Grandad (*giving the handle to Doris*) Kenneth told me to pull it towards me. (*He moves to go indoors*)

Kenneth Me?!

Grandad (*as he passes him*) Yes, you did.

Doris (*to Kenneth*) That's two pounds you owe me for a new latch.

At this point Mrs Morris comes into her garden with a basket full of washing, which she begins to peg on the line

And your breakfasts are on the table.

Ken goes into the house and Gareth goes into the loo

Doris is about to follow Ken when Mrs Morris calls to her

Mrs Morris Nice morning.

Doris (*not seeing her at first*) Oh, Audrey. Beautiful.

Mrs Morris Big day in your house today then.

Doris Yes. I'll be glad to see tomorrow though.

Mrs Morris A lot of work for one day, isn't it?

Doris And a lot of money too.

Mrs Morris But it's Registry Office, isn't it?

Doris No. St Mary's in Duke Street.

Mrs Morris (*so shocked she drops a piece of washing*) It's ... it's a white wedding then?

Doris (*proud*) Yes.

Mrs Morris (*she can't quite believe this*) A white wedding?

Doris (*annoyed at her disbelief*) A white wedding.

Mrs Morris (*realizing she might have over stepped the mark, she tries to put things right*) Oh, nice girl mind, Shirley. They've got somewhere to live have they?

Doris They're coming to live here with us.

Mrs Morris Oh there you are then—in the front room is it?

Doris Well, they offered them their front room but Gareth said they'd prefer living in with us. I'll be honest with you — I wasn't fussy on the idea to begin with. I mean, I know Shirley looks a small girl but eat, God help us. She comes to tea every Sunday as it is now — and if I didn't keep an eye on her then she'd eat me out of house and home.

Mrs Morris Still it's a start for them — that's the main thing. Had a bit of an accident, have you? (*Nodding to the handle in Doris's hand*)

Doris My father just pulled it off.

Mrs Morris How is he now, any better?

Doris (*shaking her head*) He hasn't been the same since my mother died if you ask me.

Mrs Morris Still grieving, is he?

Doris Well, between me and you — he's taken to the bottle now.

Mrs Morris He's always been a man with a thirst though, hasn't he?

Doris Yes but he's never drunk like he's drinking now. He thinks we don't know about it but he hides the bottles everywhere. Last week our toilet flush was jammed, and when our Reg went to have a look at it, there was a small bottle of gin, wedged down between the ballcock.

Mrs Morris Never! Oh he must be missing her awful.

Doris Grief will make you do funny things, you know. I remember when Reg's father died — his mother just about went off her head. She was convinced he'd come back as the budgie. For three years she believed it was her husband, until one morning she got up and the bloody thing had laid an egg. She was all right after that.

Mrs Morris Oh it's awful losing somebody.

Doris Yes. It's not going to be easy for me losing Gareth. Especially now he's earning good money.

Mrs Morris That's not the same though really, is it? Losing them to get married and losing them when they die.

Doris I suppose not. (*She makes to go back into the house*) Sometimes marriage can be much more tragic.

Doris has left the latch on the garden fence. Mrs Morris calls her to hand it to her

Mrs Morris Hey, you forgot this, look.

Doris turns and takes it from her. As she goes to leave again, Mrs Morris grabs her arm

I didn't know until Mrs Matthews told me yesterday that the wedding was today. I thought it was *next* Saturday.

Doris Well, it was going to be, but me and Reg have booked to go with British Rail on one of those mystery trips.

Mrs Morris Oh, where are you going?

Doris Blackpool.

Mrs Morris You know, I've never been there.

Doris We haven't either — that's why we booked.

There is a pause

Mrs Morris What time's the wedding?

Doris Twelve o'clock. I can't see Shirley getting there much before half-past though. She's never on time. Her mother reckons she was a ten-month pregnancy.

Mrs Morris (*amazed*) Ten months? Never, she must have had her dates wrong.

Doris That's what I said, but she wouldn't have it. You can't tell that family nothing.

Without looking at Mrs Morris she offers her a cigarette but takes the packet away as Mrs Morris reaches to take one

They're all the same, all of them, from the biggest right down to the littlest. It's our Gareth I feel sorry for, marrying into a family like that. (*She strikes a match*) That's why I'm glad in a way they're going to live here with us. I'm not going to interfere with them. (*She lights her cigarette*) I've told them, you can have the run of the house, I said. (*On the word "run" she gestures towards the house with the hand that holds the match, which is still lit*)

As she waves her hand back she tosses the match over the fence into Mrs Morris's garden. Mrs Morris looks at her in total disbelief. Doris hasn't stopped talking during any of this and continues her speech. Mrs Morris disappears briefly, we hear her stamping her foot on the match three or four times. When she re-appears she is holding the dead match boldly between her finger and thumb

Well, it's only fair, isn't it? They've got to feel as if it's their own home haven't they. And they wouldn't have been able to do that if they'd gone to live with her lot. Her mother wouldn't let them have the freedom they'll have living here with me. And they would have had to share a bedroom with her younger sister if they'd gone to live there. Well, it's not right is it? A young married couple wants a bit of privacy, don't they? A room where they can close the door and be alone together.

All this time Mrs Morris is waiting for Doris to look in her direction so that she can make her point about the match.

Oh and her father's a funny bugger too. I know he can't help it, but he's gone all nasty inside since he's had to have that wooden leg. But, putting all things aside, they're a pretty nasty lot all around. (*She turns to Mrs Morris*) Do you know them at all?

Mrs Morris Shirley's mother and me are second cousins. (*She slings the dead match over Doris's side of the fence and returns to her washing*)

Doris (*trying to cover her embarrassment*) Lovely day for a wedding though, don't you think? (*She drags on her cigarette then decides she doesn't like the taste and throws it into the bucket which is outside the loo*)

As she does this, Grandad comes into the garden holding up a white shirt which has a large hole burned into the back of it

Grandad Doris. Have you aired this shirt? Look at it.

Doris (*snatching it from him*) It's burnt through. Who did that?
Grandad I don't know. It was on the stool in front of the fire.

Mrs Morris picks up her washing basket and goes into her house

Doris Look at it. It's no good now. You'll have to put your new one on.
Grandad Where is it?
Doris Behind the fish tank in the front room.
Grandad Right.

He salutes and goes back into the house

Doris looks at the hole again then wanders over to the bench. She sits

Doris (*calling*) Gareth?
Gareth (*from inside the loo*) What?
Doris It's ten to ten.
Gareth All right.

Kenneth comes out of house and makes for the toilet

I'm in here.

Kenneth turns and almost swears. He sees Doris

Kenneth Having five are you?
Doris It's ten I should be having not five. And why didn't you keep an eye on this shirt instead of just sitting there feeding your face watching it burn.
Kenneth I suppose you're going to blame me for that as well now, are you?
Doris Well you must have smelt it scorching.
Kenneth I did, but I thought it was the bacon.
Doris Are you trying to say I scorched the bacon?
Kenneth No. (*He puts his left leg on the arm of the bench*) Burnt it. It was so crisp, I had a bacon butty and I got splinters in my mouth.
Doris Well I can't do everything. I haven't stopped this morning yet. This is the first time I've sat down since I got up.

Kenneth moves away DR

And you ought to know better too.
Kenneth What do you mean?
Doris Getting our Gareth in a state.
Kenneth *I* didn't get him in a state.
Doris I suppose he drank all he did without any help from you.
Kenneth I bought my round the same as everyone else.
Doris Only one round he needed. (*Sotto voce*) You know our Gareth can't drink.
Kenneth It was his stag night, Mam. He was suppose to get drunk.
Doris He was suppose to have a good time. It's you who can't have a good time unless you get drunk.
Kenneth Are you going to go on at me today? (*Sitting on the arm of the bench*) Isn't today going to be an exception?

Doris Listen to you and I'm always going on at you. (*After a slight pause*) You've got that lad's ring safe, have you?

Kenneth (*sighing*) Yes.

Doris I can't understand why he asked you to be his best man anyway.

He turns to look at her

Oh I know he's your brother—but after the mess you made of your cousin's wedding, I wouldn't trust you again.

Kenneth I thought I made a good best man. I made them laugh.

Doris You didn't make Auntie Alice laugh—or me either for that matter. I've never been so embarrassed and ashamed in all my life. She hasn't spoken a word since. She had a stroke two days after, you know that don't you? Shock, the doctor said it was. Shock! And we all know what brought that on, don't we?

Kenneth Well everybody else enjoyed it.

Doris Yes, but *she* was standing next to you when you did it.

Kenneth Well I didn't think to look who I was standing next to.

Doris You're missing the point, Kenneth. The point is you should not have streaked at all. And have you got a proper speech to say? Or are you going to make it up on the spur of the moment and make a mess of it like last time?

Kenneth (*after a pause as he slides down to sit next to her on the bench*) You don't think much of me, do you?

Doris I'd think a lot more of you if you weren't so wild. You should be cooling down now. Twenty-five you are not fifteen. You haven't grown up proper that's what's the matter with you. It's you who should be settling down not our Gareth.

Kenneth How can I settle down when I haven't even got a job.

Doris Look for one like Gareth did. (*After a slight pause*) I always thought you'd get married before him.

Kenneth Can I help it if I'm cleverer than he is?

Reg comes out of the house with two mugs of tea. He has a large plaster on his right cheek

Reg You're out here then.

Doris immediately spots the plaster

Doris What the hell have you done to your face?

Reg Cut myself shaving, that's all.

Doris (*going to him*) Cut yourself shaving? You've got about a yard and a half of plaster there. Is it all right?

Reg It's stopped bleeding anyway.

Doris Well you are going to look lovely in the wedding photos you are, aren't you? Between you with that plaster and Shirley's father and his wooden leg you'll look like the bloody Pirates of Penzance.

Reg (*checking his reflection in the kitchen window*) It doesn't look that bad, does it?

Doris Trust you to go and do that this morning. I suppose there's blood all over my towel now is there?

Reg No. I was very careful. (*He looks at Kenneth and winks*) I made sure the blood all dripped very neatly down the drain without even touching the sides.

Kenneth laughs, unseen by Doris

Doris You know, Reg, sometimes I get the feeling you take the mickey out of me.

Reg What have I said now?

Doris (*sitting back on the bench*) Nothing!

Kenneth I'm going to get changed then. (*He gets up and moves towards the kitchen door*)

Doris (*calling after him*) Your button-hole's in the bowl in the middle-room.

Kenneth Ay, OK.

He goes into the house

Reg goes to Doris on the bench. He offers her a mug

Doris What's that, tea?

Reg Yes.

Doris Two sugars?

Reg Yes.

Doris And plenty of milk?

Reg Yes.

Doris (*sipping it*) It's too strong.

He holds his hand out to take it back

No go on it's all right I'll drink it.

Reg sits next to her on the bench. They both sip tea. After a pause Doris brushes the grass with her foot

I thought you said you cut this grass, Reg.

Reg I did.

Doris Well it looks the same to me.

Reg I'll cut it again next week.

Doris You can't, we're in Blackpool.

Reg The week after then.

There is a pause

Doris Reg? (*She slips her arm under his*)

Reg looks slightly cautious

Have you ever wished we had daughters?

Reg (*looking perplexed*) No.

Doris Why?

He shrugs his shoulders and shakes his head

I'd have liked a daughter, Reg.

Reg You should have told me twenty years ago.

Doris Or two would have been nice.

Reg What's the matter with the two you've got?

Doris Nothing, except they're boys, and they're not the same somehow. It's times like this I'd have liked a girl. Helping to arrange things. Helping to choose materials and colours. Helping her into her wedding dress—just like Shirley's mother is doing now I expect. Giving her a kiss before we left for the church. You can't do that with boys. You can't tell them that you wish them everything in the world, and that you're going to miss them—or what a mother feels inside. You can't say that to boys. Well, not to our boys anyway.

Reg You can to Gareth.

Doris Do you think so?

He nods

Oh, I don't know. (*She thinks for a moment*) Do you remember the morning we got married, Reg?

Reg Like it was yesterday. It poured down all day. It was the wettest Tuesday in seventeen years.

Doris (*taking her arm from under his*) It was a Monday. We got married on a Monday.

Reg Was it?

Doris You were right about the rain though.

Reg Was it a Monday?

Doris Bank Holiday Monday.

Reg (*after thinking about it*) Ay, that's right. (*He sips his tea*) I've got to be honest with you though, Doris. I didn't think we'd still be together after all these years.

Doris (*shocked*) Didn't you?

Reg I remember saying to my mother before we left for the registry office. "Don't worry," I said. "Six months it will last at the most."

Doris Is that all you gave us?

Reg (*smiling*) Six months. I was sure it wouldn't last more than that. (*He looks at her*) Funny how wrong you can be isn't it?

Doris Not really. (*Grabbing him above the knee*) I had my grips on you and I wasn't going to let you go. You were sexy then, and you couldn't keep your hands off me.

Reg (*laughing*) Yeah.

Doris (*after a slight pause*) Any regrets Reg?

Reg Well . . .

Doris Truth now.

Reg (*thinking it over*) No.

Doris Honest?

He nods. A thought strikes her

You've always been honest with me Reg, haven't you? What I mean is, throughout our marriage, have you ever lied to me deliberately?

Reg (*looking rather uncomfortable*) No, I don't think so.

Doris doesn't altogether believe him

Doris Well, if I ask you something now will you tell me the truth?
Reg Yes.
Doris Honest?
Reg Honest.
Doris (*after a long pause*) How was the bacon this morning?
Reg (*not quite sure if he heard correctly*) Pardon?
Doris I said, how was the bacon this morning?
Reg (*still not absolutely sure*) Is that it? Is that the question?
Doris Yes. Come on tell me.
Reg (*thinking carefully about it*) Crisp.
Doris (*over the moon*) Thank you, Reg. (*She kisses him on the cheek*) That's all I wanted to know.
Reg (*not quite believing all this*) Are you all right?

She nods

Do you want me to get you two Librium or something?
Doris No I'm fine.
Reg Are you sure?
Doris Yes.
Reg (*looking at her in a very strange way*) I'm going to get ready then. (*He stands and is about to leave*) Are you coming?
Doris No, you go in, I'll be there in a minute.

He moves towards the house

Reg?

He turns

You think I can tell Gareth then?
Reg Tell him what?
Doris (*pausing slightly*) Nothing. It's all right. Go on.

He goes into the house

Doris relaxes back on the bench for a moment. She is deep in thought. Then she speaks

Gareth?
Gareth (*from inside the loo*) What?
Doris (*after a pause*) Nothing— it's all right. (*She stands and walks half-way between the loo and the house. She stops and hesitates*) Gareth?
Gareth (*still inside the loo*) What?
Doris (*still she can't bring herself to say what she wants*) It's all right it doesn't matter. (*She walks towards the house but she can't go in either. She turns and walks up to the loo*) Gareth?
Gareth (*after a pause*) What?

She fights hard to say what she wants but loses. She is almost crying

Doris Call me when you've finished.

She is obviously upset and she rushes into the house

The Lights fade to a Black-out

SCENE 2

The same. 10.30 pm the same night

The CURTAIN *rises on Shirley sitting on the garden bench. After about three or four seconds, the back door opens. The sound of the party which is going on inside the house becomes louder. It must be noted that the sound level within the house increases and decreases if and when the kitchen door is opened.*

Grandad comes out of the house carrying a large bottle of gin. He is drunk and walks with difficulty towards the toilet. He can't seem to walk in the direction he intends. He misses the toilet door and swings around almost immediately, not seeing Shirley, or her him. He aims once more but again misses the door and about-turns so rapidly that he loses his balance and literally falls into the loo. This walk of Grandad's could almost be described as a dance. After he has closed the door behind him . . .

Gareth steps out of the house. He is wearing a dark suit. As he closes the door there is a roar of laugher from inside the house. He strolls to the bottom of the garden where he sees Shirley

Gareth Oh, so you're out here then. I wondered where you were.
Shirley I came out for some air.
Gareth Yeah, it is stuffy.

There is another roar of laughter from inside the house, then they begin to sing

Shirley They seem to be enjoying themselves.
Gareth Aren't you? (*He turns to face her*)
Shirley Course I am.

He moves and sits right of her on the bench. He takes her hand

Gareth You looked lovely today, Shirl. I don't think I've ever seen you look so lovely.
Shirley Thanks. You looked pretty smart yourself.
Gareth Were you nervous?
Shirley I don't think so.
Gareth I was.
Shirley Yes I know.
Gareth Did it show?
Shirley Now and then.
Gareth When?
Shirley In your speech.
Gareth At the reception?
Shirley Yes.
Gareth I did my best.

Shirley Of course you did.
Gareth Perhaps I should have written it down.
Shirley Yes.

There is a pause

Gareth It was all right though, was it?

She looks at him

My speech.
Shirley (*smiling*) Yes.
Gareth As good as Kenneth's?
Shirley Better.
Gareth Really?
Shirley You want the truth?
Gareth Yes.
Shirley No.

Gareth is a little hurt and disappointed. He turns away slightly

Why do you always compare yourself with him?
Gareth I didn't realize I did.
Shirley You always want to be better than he is. Or as good as anyway.
Gareth I admire him.
Shirley Why?
Gareth I don't know. Because he's older perhaps.
Shirley No that's not it.
Gareth Because he's all the things I'm not then.
Shirley Or all the things you want to be?
Gareth Yeah, perhaps that's it.
Shirley (*turning slightly away from him*) What do you want to be like *him* for?
Gareth Well why not?
Shirley He's no provider.
Gareth He's got confidence.
Shirley But no sense of responsibility.
Gareth People like him.
Shirley He's immature.
Gareth 'Cause he's got plenty of personality.
Shirley And selfish.
Gareth And handsome.
Shirley And lazy.
Gareth And funny.
Shirley And good-looking.
Gareth And wicked.
Shirley And sexy.
Gareth And ... what?
Shirley (*realizing what she has said*) What?
Gareth (*facing her*) Did you say sexy?

Shirley (*trying to cover up*) No.
Gareth I thought you said sexy.
Shirley No. *You* said he was sexy.
Gareth (*after a slight pause*) Did I?
Shirley (*taking his hand again*) But do you know what he's not?

He shakes his head

Sincere. When you tell me something nice I believe you. With Ken, he just turns on the charm.
Gareth But people like him.
Shirley People like you.
Gareth Do they?

They look into each other's eyes

Shirley Well I'm people aren't I?
Gareth I love you, Shirl. I love you and I'm glad you're having my baby.

Gareth kisses her. The toilet flushes

Grandad comes out of the loo. As he closes the door behind him he sees them. Trying not to make too much noise he eases backwards towards R. *As he does this he almost falls over the bucket*

Gareth and Shirley hear this and release each other

Grandad Kicked the bucket. (*He laughs at his own joke*)

Gareth and Shirley see the bottle of gin. Grandad quickly tries to hide it in the empty bucket

Gareth Enjoying yourself, Grandad?
Grandad (*going over to them*) Yes. I won't ask you the same though.
Gareth Shirley wanted some air.
Grandad I bet she did. Hey, you'd better not let Kenneth see you.
Gareth Why's that, Grandad?
Grandad Well hell, he's only been married a day. He's not going to like it if he comes out here and sees you kissing his bride.
Gareth (*laughing*) No Grandad, you've got it wrong, Shirley married me not Kenneth.
Grandad (*shocked*) Married you?
Gareth Yes, me. Gareth.
Grandad Not Kenneth?
Gareth That's right.

Gareth thinks this is funny. Shirley isn't so sure

He's drunk.
Grandad (*thinking this is funny now too*) Oh hell, I thought she married the other one.

The back door opens and we hear Doris

Doris (*off*) Well she shouldn't be up at this time of night anyway—not a woman in her state of health.

Doris comes into the garden and takes the bucket which is near the back door and hands it to Reg inside

As she does this Grandad watches his bottle of gin disappear into the house along with the bucket

Here you are, Reg, take this bucket.
Reg (*off*) No, I'm not seeing to her.
Doris Take it Reg, will you!
Reg (*off*) She's your auntie not mine.
Doris Take it!

He does

I can't see to her, it's turning my stomach. (*She comes into the garden*) Arthur should have known better and taken her home long before now.

Gareth is sitting forward on the bench, temporarily hiding Shirley from Doris

(*To Gareth*) And all them ports didn't help either.
Gareth What's the matter in there then?
Doris Auntie Alice has lost control of her bowels. I told them what would happen. She's been breaking wind all night but Arthur wouldn't believe me—he kept saying it was the dog.

Gareth laughs at this and leans backwards on the bench revealing Shirley

Oh ... hello Shirley luv. Everything all right?
Shirley Yes thanks.
Doris Good.

She looks at Grandad who can hardly stand

And what are you doing out here?
Grandad   My little girl
 (*singing*)   Pink and white as peaches and cream, is she.
                     My little girl,
                     Is half ...

He has pitched it far too high and cannot reach the high note, but he does attempt it

Doris Take him in quick, Gareth before he breaks a blood vessel.
Gareth (*leading him towards the house*) Come on, Grandad.
Gareth Hey ... hey, they used to call me Caruso when I was younger, you know.
Gareth Caruso? Who's he?
Grandad You mean to tell me you've never heard of Caruso? He had the finest voice this side of Lynn.
Gareth Lynn?
Grandad (*shouting*) Vera Lynn, what's the matter with you.

Gareth bursts out laughing as he takes him inside the house

Doris watches them go. There is a pause as Doris joins Shirley on the bench

Doris Well you've had a lovely day, Shirley. Lovely. Your mother did you proud.

Shirley Yes. Pity about the photographer though.

Doris It was his own fault. Common sense should have told him not to lean that far over the balcony.

Shirley He wanted to get an overhead picture of us.

Doris He cracked the font. I saw it with my own eyes. Right down the centre it was. Good job he had another camera in the car.

Reg opens the back door and calls

Reg (*off*) Doris.
Doris What?
Reg (*off*) Where's the Parazone?
Doris Under the sink!

Reg closes the door

Well, I hope you'll settle in here, Shirley.

Shirley Yes.

Doris I want us to live like one big happy family. You are to use this house as if it's your own.

Shirley Thank you.

Doris Oh and feel free to wash the dishes any time they're dirty. (*She laughs at her little joke. The fact is she wasn't really joking*)

At this point, Gareth comes out of the house and goes into the loo unseen by Doris and Shirley

No, seriously now though, in case you need it and I'm not here I keep the vacuum cleaner in the cupboard under the stairs. If there's anything you want to know, Shirley don't be afraid to ask — that's what I'm here for — to help you. And if you get in any sort of trouble handling the money, just let me know and we'll do the shopping together. But don't think I'm interfering mind. I only want to help you — put you on your feet.

Shirley Thank you.

Doris Oh and I do the washing every Monday like clockwork.

Shirley Right.

Doris So you can do yours on a Tuesday. Until the baby comes of course, then I'll get Reg to put the washing machine out the shed so you can do all the nappies out there. Not that I mind you doing them in the kitchen — but it's Reg see. He's a bit fussy like that.

The back door opens and Reg screams

Reg (*off*) Doris, for God's sake, I want you.
Doris All right, all right. He'll keep on till I go.

Reg closes the door

Are you coming in?

Shirley No, I'll stay out here for a bit.

Doris nods and goes indoors

Shirley sighs heavily. She walks over to have a closer look at the shed

The back door opens and Kenneth sneaks out

Kenneth (*not drunk, but almost*) There she is.

Shirley turns to see him

Shirley Oh it's you.

Kenneth Course it's me—who did you think it was?

Shirley You're drunk.

Kenneth Course I'm drunk—everybody's drunk.

Shirley (*coming back to sit on the bench*) I'm not.

Kenneth Well you should be.

Shirley Why?

Kenneth Why? Now that's a good question. (*He looks at her for a moment. He puts his left leg up on the arm of the bench*) So ... you're a married woman now then.

Shirley I'm your sister-in-law now, yes.

Kenneth Do I get to (*with a French accent*) "kiss ze bride"?

Shirley No.

Kenneth Why?

Shirley (*after a slight pause*) It's in the best interest you didn't.

Kenneth In whose best interest?

Shirley (*after a pause*) Gareth's.

Kenneth (*swaying slightly*) I know he's my brother, right? (*He points his finger at her*) But you knew he was my brother too.

Shirley You knew I was drunk.

Kenneth You like me anyway whether you're sober or whether you're drunk.

Shirley I was drunk and you took advantage of that.

Kenneth It wasn't all one-sided.

Shirley No I know, but I can't let it happen again, I just can't.

Kenneth I only want to kiss you.

Shirley You said that the last time.

Kenneth (*smiling as he takes his foot from the bench*) Did I?

Shirley And you know what that led to.

Kenneth You sound as though you regret it.

Shirley I do.

Kenneth You're a liar.

Shirley immediately stands

Shirley (*after a pause*) I'm going in. (*She rushes past him*)

As she does this he grabs her by the arm

Kenneth No don't go. Please? I'm sorry.

He puts her to sit on the bench, then climbs over the bench

Shirley Don't you have any scruples?

Kenneth (*putting his hands around her waist*) I think I just lost them on the edge of that. Once more please, for old time's sake.

Shirley (*tempted*) No.

Kenneth I only want to kiss you.

Shirley As a sister-in-law?

He shake his head

Then I can't.

He moves away down L

Kenneth What are you afraid of? (*Looking briefly towards the house*) Not that someone will see us?

She shakes her head

What then?

Shirley Of what I'll feel inside. I'm married to Gareth, your brother. I'm going to live in this house with both of you. It's going to be difficult enough for me as it is. I can't let it happen again, I can't.

Kenneth I'm not asking you to.

Shirley You don't know what you're asking.

Kenneth I only want to kiss you.

Shirley But it's more than that.

Kenneth (*tenderly*) Is it?

Shirley Of course it is. (*Not at all sure how to proceed with the following conversation*) Do you remember when it happened? Gareth was in hospital with his tonsils.

Kenneth Gillian Booth's engagement party.

Shirley "Go," he said. "It'll be all right, Kenneth will be there," he said. Little did he know.

Kenneth It's a bit late to have any hang-ups about it now.

Shirley Do you think so? How long has Gillian has engaged?

Kenneth (*thinking about it*) I don't know. About three months.

Shirley He trusts me. I can't say he trusts you because he doesn't even consider you.

He moves and stands directly behind her, his body next to hers. As he says his line he slips his hand down and touches her bottom

Kenneth I'm not asking you to do it again.

Shirley (*snapping*) Hey! What do you think I am?

Kenneth Sssshhhhh!

Shirley (*still shouting*) Who the hell do you think you are?

Kenneth Someone will come out.

Shirley You think that you're so bloody good-looking that one smile and a wink from you and I'm yours. You think that you can bowl me over with all that charm of yours and all that bloody rubbish you spout to all the other girls. What makes you think that you're any different from anyone else?

There is a slight pause. She kisses him. After she kisses him she turns away down R

I'm three months' pregnant.

Kenneth Yes, I know. Gareth told me.

Shirley I take it back. I take back all I said. You wanted a kiss and you've had one, now go back inside, please? Before I do it again.

Kenneth turns and goes to her

Kenneth What's the matter? What's the matter with you?

Shirley I'm married to Gareth, right?

He nods

Right.

Kenneth (*taking her in his arms*) Hey, come on.

Shirley Oh I could kick myself.

Kenneth What for?

Shirley (*kissing him again*) I hate you. (*And she kisses him again*) I really do hate you.

He kisses her

You shouldn't have done that, Ken, you shouldn't have.

He tries to kiss her again but she breaks away and moves down R. *By this time her emotions are totally confused*

I'm three months' pregnant did I tell you?

Kenneth Yes.

Shirley Yes I thought I did. (*A slight pause*) I'm married to Gareth.

Kenneth But?

Shirley You're no provider, Ken. You've no sense of responsibility.

Kenneth And?

Shirley You're lazy.

Kenneth (*moving away upstage to the kitchen window*) If you go on saying those things you'll convince yourself.

Shirley I am married to Gareth.

Kenneth (*putting his right hand up to rest on the wall of the house as he peers in*) And you're three months' pregnant.

Shirley Yes. (*A slight pause*) Doesn't that mean anything to you?

Kenneth (*after thing about it for a moment*) I'm going to be an uncle?

Shirley Gillian Booth's engagement party.

The penny drops. It suddenly dawns on him. He turns to face her

Kenneth You mean ... (*He points to her stomach and nods*) You mean, the baby's my baby?

Shirley I think it might be.

He rushes to her and takes her arm and gently puts her to sit on the bench

Kenneth What do you mean, you think it might be? Don't you know?

Shirley (*shaking her head*) I went to visit Gareth before I came to Gillian's party. He was off the main ward—in a small room of his own. (*She slowly looks up to him*)

Kenneth You mean you, (*he nods his head*) with Gareth?

Shirley Yes.

Kenneth Before you——

Shirley Yes——

Kenneth With me at——

Shirley Yes. I was drunk. You made me drunk.

Kenneth (*frustrated and annoyed, moving away down* R) Why didn't you tell me before? (*He runs his fingers through his hair*)

Shirley I don't know why I'm telling you now. I don't like you—I never have.

Kenneth How can you say you don't like me when we——

Shirley I told you—I was drunk. (*She pauses*) Gareth's ready for marriage. He's a good provider. He'll be good in the house.

Kenneth But lousy in bed?

Shirley No, not lousy. (*She turns away as she says rather quietly*) He's just not as good as you are, that's all.

There is a pause

Kenneth So what happens now?

Shirley Nothing. I'm married to Gareth so I'm his wife. I'm having his baby and as far as I'm concerned it's his. (*Going back to sit on the bench*) There's a fifty-fifty chance of me being right, anyway.

Kenneth There's a fifty-fifty chance of you being wrong too. Is that why you married him and not me—because he's a good provider?

Shirley It's why I didn't marry you, yes.

Kenneth So you admit you could have then? What I mean is—you can't hate me that much, if at all, if you could have married me.

Shirley I don't love you.

Kenneth And Gareth?

Shirley (*after a slight pause*) I will eventually.

Kenneth But what happens until then?

Shirley (*sighing*) I don't know.

Kenneth The spirit might be strong but the flesh is weak.

Shirley (*snapping again as she rises to her feet*) You think I can't say no to you, don't you? You think because you had me once, when I was drunk, you can have me again and again and again.

Kenneth I think you married the wrong brother, that's all.

Shirley What if I have? I'll never want for anything. Not with Gareth.

Kenneth No, he'll give you everything you want . . . except me.

Shirley I don't want you.

Kenneth I think you do. Not now perhaps, not at this moment, but you do, and there's nothing you can do about that. Whatever it is two people need to make it together, Shirl we've got it—and that will always draw us together—like magnets.

Shirley You're so bloody cock-sure of yourself, aren't you?

Kenneth Only when I know I'm right.
Shirley Yes well this time you're wrong.

She storms past him but as she does this he grabs her and kisses her violently. The kiss is long and hard

　Grandad comes out of the house, singing, with his bottle. He walks towards the toilet but sees Kenneth and Shirley still kissing. He sings a little louder

They spring apart

Grandad (*singing*)
　　　　　　　　Girls were made to love and kiss,
　　　　　　　　And who am I to interefere with this,
　　　　　　　　Does it pay, who can say, I ...

He attempts the high note but again nothing comes out. Suddenly he realizes that it's Kenneth kissing Shirley

　Hello, hello, hello, what's going on here? (*Imitating a policeman*) What's going on here then. (*He laughs*) What's going on here. Do you get it? (*He bends his knees*) Get it look?

Kenneth and Shirley look at each other then force a laugh

Kenneth ⎫
Shirley ⎭ (*together*) Yes.
Grandad I don't. Where's Gareth?
Shirley (*nervous*) Gareth?
Grandad He's not going to like this, you know.

Shirley looks at Kenneth

Kenneth (*to the rescue*) Like what, Grandad?
Grandad I saw you kissing Shirley.
Kenneth (*improvising madly*) Well ... there's ... er ... there's nothing wrong in that is there? I mean, a man can kiss his wife, can't he?

Shirley looks at him. She can't believe what he is saying

Grandad (*he can't believe his ears either*) His wife? *Your* wife? I thought she was Gareth's wife.
Shirley I am——

Kenneth nudges her

　--not Gareth's wife.
Grandad (*to Shirley*) You're not?
Kenneth No. Who told you that, Grandad?

Grandad thinks for a moment as he looks towards the back door, trying to work it out

Grandad Gareth did.
Kenneth Ah he was having you on.
Grandad Having me on?

Kenneth That's right—pulling your leg.

Grandad Pulling my leg. (*He thinks for a moment then laughs as he accepts the situation*) I thought it was you who got married Ken, I didn't think it was our Gareth somehow. (*He puts his bottle of gin to his lips but finds it empty*) Oh, empty. I'm just going in for a minute.

He is almost at the kitchen door when he stops to look at the couple. He winks at them and then drags one foot on the floor like an aroused bull. Kenneth and Shirley laugh with Grandad, but their laugh is uncomfortable. Kenneth laughs the loudest. Shirley puts her heel on to his toe and presses down firmly. Kenneth's laughter subtly turns to shrieks of pain

Grandad goes inside

When he has disappeared, Kenneth pushes Shirley away

Shirley What did you tell him that for?

Kenneth (*nursing his foot*) He's drunk. He won't remember anything in the morning.

Shirley What if he does?

Kenneth He won't.

There is a pause

Shirley Do you think we'd better go in as well.

Kenneth OK, if you want to.

Shirley We can't go in together. You go in first.

Kenneth All right. (*He doesn't move*)

Shirley (*after she's realized*) Well go on then.

Kenneth No. I don't want to go in yet.

Shirley Well I'm not going in first.

Kenneth Why?

Shirley Because I'm not.

Kenneth Tell me why then.

Shirley Because that's why.

Kenneth Look, why don't you come out and say it.

Shirley Say what?

Kenneth (*going to her*) That you don't really want to go in there, (*he points to the house*) because you'd rather stay out here, with me.

Shirley Oh you are a bastard.

He pulls her towards him and kisses her again. Suddenly the back door opens and they release each other

Reg, Doris, Grandad, Mrs Morris and possibly a few extras come out of the house dancing the conga. They dance zig-zag across the stage, and on their way back they pick up Shirley, and Kenneth tags on to the end. They finally dance into the house, and the last person to enter should be Kenneth, who kicks the door closed, preferably to the music

After the door is closed and the music and noise of the party have completely faded, the toilet door slowly opens and Gareth comes out. He is obviously

upset. He doesn't really know what to do. Suddenly he makes a definite
move towards the back door, but then equally as suddenly stops short of it.
He cannot bring himself to go inside. He moves to the window and looks in.
He pauses then slowly turns and walks back into the loo. After he has closed
the door . . .

The Lights fade to a Black-out

ACT II

The same. A very hot August, midday

The CURTAIN *comes up on Reg who is on all fours cutting the grass,* R. *Grandad is fast asleep in a deck-chair which is to the right of the bench. The "News of the World" or some local rag is up over his head completely covering his face. Reg stops cutting the grass for a moment and stretches his back. He notices that Grandad is sleeping*

Reg Don't go to sleep now, Dad, dinner's almost ready.

There is silence

Dad!

Grandad snores. Doris calls, off, from the kitchen to Shirley who is somewhere upstairs

Doris (*off*) Shirley? Shirley! Leave the bedrooms for now and come and give me a hand with the dinner.

Grandad snores again

Reg Dad!

Mrs Morris comes into her garden and feels the washing on her line. She spots Reg

Mrs Morris Another warm one.

Reg (*at first wondering where the voice was coming from, then seeing her*) Pardon?

Mrs Morris I said it's another warm one.

Reg Oh, yes.

Mrs Morris Day off today is it, Reg?

Reg Ay. Funeral.

Mrs Morris (*coming to the wall*) Oh. Somebody died?

Reg Well yes. Doris's Auntie Alice.

Mrs Morris Oh she's dead, is she? Sorry to hear that. Still, she must have been well into her seventies so she was a good old age. Sudden was it?

Reg Last Monday afternoon.

Mrs Morris Pity. What time's the funeral?

Reg One o'clock from the house.

Mrs Morris Very nice too. (*Pointing to Grandad*) Is *he* going?

Reg We're all going. Except Shirley of course.

Mrs Morris I don't blame her either. A funeral's no place for a pregnant woman — it's never looked right to me somehow. How is she anyway, I haven't seen her for a fortnight.

Reg She's all right.

Mrs Morris No trouble yet is there?

Reg Trouble?

Mrs Morris With the old blood pressure. Mine used to go up and down like a lift.

Grandad snores again

Sleeping is he?

Reg No, he always makes that noise when he's reading.

Mrs Morris He's not reading, is he?

Reg Yes.

Mrs Morris But the paper's up over his head.

Reg Ay, he's very short-sighted.

Mrs Morris (*for a moment she can't quite work it out, then she decides he must be joking*) Go on, Reg you're having me on.

Reg I wouldn't dare.

Doris comes out of the house

Doris Go and have your dinner now, Reg while Shirley's putting it out. (*Crossing to Mrs Morris*) It's hot, isn't it?

Reg goes inside leaving the shears outside the back door. He leans them against the wall

Mrs Morris I was just saying to Reg it was another warm one.

Doris It's too hot for a funeral.

Mrs Morris I hope it's raining when they bury me. Well not so much rain as a fine drizzle.

Doris looks at her in amazement

Well, we've all got our little quirks.

Doris Cremated I'm going to be anyway.

Mrs Morris Oh no I don't want that. I never want to be cremated.

Doris It's cleaner.

Mrs Morris No, I don't want to be burnt. I can't stand heat anyway, I come out in a rash. (*Showing Doris her bare arm*) I've got it now look in this weather.

Doris (*nodding in agreement*) I'm just about frying myself in this dress — and black draws the heat, don't it?

Mrs Morris Yes. (*After a slight pause*) Hey, I didn't know until Reg said now that she'd gone.

Doris Who?

Mrs Morris Your Auntie Alice.

Doris It was no surprise.

Mrs Morris (*sounding almost disappointed*) Oh, and Reg said it was sudden.

Doris It was, but we half expected it. Well I mean she never really got over that stroke.

Mrs Morris Did she ever speak at all after the stroke?

Doris Not a word. The only thing she ever managed to do after that was belch—and when she realized she could do that there was no stopping her. She was belching for everything. She could do it at will in the end.

Mrs Morris (*after thinking about it for some time*) I thought her son's name was Arthur.

Doris (*thinking about poor old Arthur*) It is.

Mrs Morris (*after a slight pause*) Well who is Will then?

Doris (*still in thought*) I don't know. (*Suddenly the word "will" has registered in her brain*) What will? Has she left a will?

Mrs Morris What are you asking me for? I don't know—I don't know everything. (*After a slight pause*) But—if you *do* ask me there's no smoke without fire—there's a will there somewhere, mark my words.

Doris (*almost to herself*) She never spent much money I know.

Mrs Morris (*shocked*) Did she have money then?

Doris Well she must have; but Arthur will have all that now of course.

Mrs Morris Unless she leaves it to Will.

Doris Will who?

Mrs Morris I don't know. The only Will I know . . . (*a scandal is beginning to hatch in her brain*) . . . is Will Pickett the chemist.

Doris What's he got to do with it?

Mrs Morris The mind boggles.

Doris What does she want to leave her money to him for?

Mrs Morris He's a married man.

Doris With four grown-up children.

Mrs Morris And an Alsatian.

Doris The mind boggles.

Mrs Morris (*frantically thinking of an excuse to leave in order to spread the news*) Listen, I've got to go in—I'm sure there's somebody knocking my front door.

She rushes off

Doris thinks it all over for a moment, then on seeing Grandad, pushes it to the back of her mind. She creeps up behind him and wickedly snatches the newspaper away from him

Doris Don't go to sleep now Dad, dinner's almost ready. (*She turns away from him and folds the paper. She suddenly becomes aware that he hasn't flinched. A horrible thought crosses her mind. She bends over to take a closer look at him*) Dad?

Slowly the old man opens his eyes. Doris moves away slightly as she realizes that everything is all right. She puts her hand to her chest as she heaves a sigh of relief

Thank God for that.

Grandad I can't stick this heat, Doris. It's too hot for me.

Doris (*her concern turning to anger*) Well you shouldn't sit in the sun if it's too warm for you.

Grandad I had to come out here. Gareth and Ken were having a go again.

Doris (*sitting on the bench*) I know, I have told them. I don't know what's the matter with our Gareth but since he's been married he's been awful moody.

Grandad Since who's been married?

Doris Gareth.

Grandad (*after a slight pause*) When did *he* get married then?

Doris Now don't start.

Grandad Did I go to that?

Doris You're not serious?

Grandad I went to Ken's wedding, I know.

Doris *Ken's* not married. Gareth is the married one.

Grandad (*trying to work it out*) Gareth?

Doris Gareth and Shirley.

Grandad (*thinking about it*) Shirley ... Shirley. That's the girl who's living in with us, is it?

Doris I think I'll have you put away.

Grandad No listen now—so it's her and Gareth then.

Doris That's right.

He nods—still not absolutely sure

I'm at my wits' end with those boys.

Grandad Throw them out. Send them packing. They'll soon come to their senses.

Doris I think things might start to come a bit better soon. Ken's got a job.

Grandad Hasn't he been working?

Doris I think you live in a dream.

Grandad Which of them works in a factory?

Doris Gareth.

Grandad That's the quiet one?

Doris Well he used to be.

Grandad And what's that Ken going to do?

Doris Drive a van. He's hiring videos—something like that.

Grandad Should be out of the house quite a bit then.

Doris I hope so. It's like bedlam in there sometimes.

Grandad You don't have to tell me I've had a guts full between the pair of them.

Doris It's not like them to quarrel all the time. They used to be so close— thick as thieves.

Grandad Well that's what comes of all living under the same roof, I suppose. I remember when me and your mother first got married—we went to live with Auntie Alice's mother and there was all hell let loose there one day because——

Doris Hey, have you heard the news about her? She's supposed to have got money, and left it all to Will Pickett the chemist.

Grandad It's not true—it's a rumour. She's been dead all of thirty years.

Doris Who?

Grandad Auntie Alice's mother.

Doris I'm talking about Auntie Alice not her bloody mother.

Grandad drags his chair nearer to Doris

Grandad Auntie Alice has left money?

Doris (*nodding*) And all to Will Pickett.

Grandad The chemist?

Doris That's right.

Grandad She didn't have two halfpennies to rub together.

Doris Oh I don't know—she never used to spend much.

Grandad No, because Arthur used to spend it all on the dogs.

Doris Arthur never kept dogs.

Grandad He used to bet on them, not keep them. (*Thinking it all over*) Will
Pickett the chemist, you said.

Doris nods

What does she want to leave her money to him for?

Doris I don't know. Perhaps there was something going on between them.

Grandad Between Auntie Alice and Will Pickett?

Doris You never know. She had a lot of prescriptions last, going off.

*At this point Gareth and Ken start arguing from inside the house. It is not a
row, their argument is ad-lib and should be heard under Grandad and Doris's
conversation*

Grandad But she was seventy-three if she was a day.

Doris And he was forty-two and married.

Grandad It must have been her money he was after.

*Kenneth comes out of the house in a bit of a temper. He thought he would be
alone out there but he sees the others. He sighs, and he takes his comb out of
the back pocket of his jeans and combs his hair in the reflection of the
kitchen window*

Doris Poor old Arthur. (*To Ken*) What was all that about in there?

Kenneth Nothing.

Doris Have you had your dinner?

Kenneth I don't want salad again.

Doris Well, you don't want a hot meal in this weather.

Kenneth We've had it every day this week.

Doris Well I bought a big lettuce and I wasn't going to waste it. I don't
know—you youngsters these days, you don't know you're born. You're
lucky you got a choice. When I was a little girl if you didn't eat what was
put in front of you, you went without.

Kenneth (*who has heard it all before*) I remember my mother——

Doris I remember my mother giving me Spotted Dick one day.

Kenneth You like Spotted Dick.

Doris Not for breakfast. But she couldn't give me nothing else because
there *was* nothing else. No bread, no milk, no nothing.

Kenneth And if we ever had——

Doris And if we ever had a joint of meat on a Sunday we thought we were in God's pocket.

Kenneth Times were hard then——

Grandad Times were hard then——

Doris Times were hard then, but I don't know, we seemed to have more fun in those days.

Reg taps the inside of the kitchen window

Reg Doris! Tell Dad to come in and have his dinner.

Reg disappears

Doris (*to Grandad*) Did you hear that?

Grandad I'm just going. (*He gets up and goes towards the house. As he passes Kenneth he gives him a look*)

Grandad goes into the house

Doris You found a black tie then?

Kenneth (*moving to the bench*) Yes, I found a black tie but it's not mine it's Gareth's.

Doris Whose tie has he got?

Kenneth Dad's.

Doris And who's got his?

Kenneth Well I must have.

Doris But you said you've got Gareth's.

Kenneth (*snapping*) Well I don't know whose it is. (*He sits next to her*)

Doris You've all got one each though, have you?

Kenneth Yes.

Doris That's all right then.

There is a pause. She looks at him

And what are you looking so miserable about? You used to be full of fun. The laughing boy of Brooks Street.

Kenneth I've cooled down.

Doris Cooled down?

Kenneth Well that's what you wanted, wasn't it? Only a couple of months ago you were reminding me of my age—telling me I should be settling down. Don't you remember?

Doris Yes I remember but—are you settling down then?

Kenneth I might be.

Doris Who is she—do I know her?

Kenneth Perhaps.

Doris Tell me who she is then?

Kenneth No.

Doris Why?

Kenneth Because I don't want to.

Doris Ashamed of us, are you? Ashamed to bring her to the house, is that it?

Kenneth (*pointing to her*) Look don't push me, OK? Just don't push me.
Doris Hey! (*She slaps her hand*) Touchy!

Kenneth looks away from her. There is a long pause

Tell me about this job you've got.
Kenneth (*after a slight pause*) Nothing *to* tell.
Doris Well is it permanent?
Kenneth Yes. As far as I know. Depends on how well I do I suppose.
Doris What's the money like?
Kenneth Works on a commission basis. The more films I hire the more money I make.
Doris Can't see it working out myself.
Kenneth Don't underestimate me. I can sell nappies to a nun if I want to.
Doris I can't see you selling anything to anyone with a face like that.
Kenneth Yeah, well all that's going to change.
Doris I'm glad to hear it.
Kenneth Now that I'm working things are going to be different.
Doris Good. And perhaps we'll have a bit more peace and quiet in the house as well.
Kenneth It's not *all* me.
Doris No I know—you're both as bad as each other. I don't know what's the matter with the pair of you. (*After a pause*) There *is* something, isn't there?

He looks at her. They stare at each other for a brief moment

Gareth comes out of the house with a black tie

Gareth Mam, Grandad wants you. (*To Kenneth*) Here you are. (*He offers Kenneth the black tie*) This is yours, isn't it?
Kenneth No, Dad's got mine!
Gareth I thought you said I had yours.
Kenneth (*hackles rising*) You've got Dad's.
Gareth Well whose has Dad got then?
Kenneth (*screaming as he rises to his feet*) Mine, mine!

Doris stands and interrupts them

Doris Hey! Now behave yourselves. The two of you.

Doris goes off into the house

There is a pause. Kenneth breaks it, calmer now·

Kenneth We'll stick to what we've got then.
Gareth Yeah, all right. (*He rolls the tie up and puts it in his pocket as he wanders round the other side of the bench*)

Another pause

Kenneth Listen— I'm sorry——
Gareth What for?

Kenneth (*nodding towards the house*) For in there. It's me—it's my fault. It's just that I'm a bit ... well, you know ... lately.

Gareth Your time of the month is it?

Kenneth laughs and a moment later Gareth joins him. Suddenly we see a brief moment of how they used to be together

Kenneth (*still laughing*) That was good. We haven't had a laugh for ages.

Together their laughter subsides. They are left looking at each other. Kenneth breaks it

Hey, I've got some good news.

Gareth Yeah, I've got some news as well. (*He pauses*) I've had the sack.

Kenneth What?

Gareth Well not the sack—same thing though. I've been made redundant.

Kenneth When?

Gareth Had the letter this morning. Two more weeks—that's all I've got left.

Kenneth (*after a slight pause*) Still, they'll pay you off. I mean I suppose you'll be all right for a couple of quid.

Gareth (*obviously lying, although Kenneth doesn't see it*) Yeah, it'll be a tidy sum, yeah.

Kenneth (*after a slight pause*) You and Shirley will be moving out then?

Gareth Just as soon as we can. Should be enough for a deposit if nothing else. (*After a pause*) What's your news?

Kenneth Er ... it's just er ...

Gareth Come on tell me.

Kenneth A job. I've got myself a job.

Gareth (*after a slight pause*) Great.

Kenneth Yeah. Forgotten what it's like to have some money in my pocket.

Gareth You've always done all right.

Kenneth Get some new clothes at last. Suit—shoes, haven't dressed up for ages.

Gareth Putting yourself back on the market then?

Kenneth Oh I wouldn't say that.

Kenneth realizes what Gareth might have meant by his last remark and looks at him. Gareth realizes what Kenneth might have meant by his and they stare at each other

I think I'd better go in. This weather gives me a headache.

They are still staring at each other

Gareth Got one now, have you?

Kenneth Yeah, a stinker.

Kenneth breaks the stare and goes into the house

The minute he shuts the back door behind him, Gareth gives way to his built-up temper and lashes out, smashing the shed window with his fist. After a few moments he brings himself together

Shirley looks out from the kitchen window. She sees Gareth and comes out into the garden

Shirley Your dinner's ready.
Gareth (*shouting at her, his back towards her*) I don't want it now—I'll have it after.
Shirley (*realizing she's picked a bad time*) All right!

She turns to go back inside the house. She stops. Gareth has turned to face her. She senses this. She turns around and sees his bleeding hand

What have you done?

Gareth looks at his hand and it is only then that he realizes he is bleeding

Gareth Nothing. It's all right, it's nothing.
Shirley Come in the house and let me dress it for you.
Gareth (*firmly*) It's all right I said.

There is a pause

Shirley Will you be gone long this afternoon?
Gareth Why?
Shirley I just wondered, that's all.
Gareth Be back about five I expect. (*After a slight pause*) You're sure you won't come?
Shirley I told you, I can't. Not looking like this. It wouldn't be right.
Gareth That's a laugh.
Shirley What is?
Gareth (*after a slight pause*) Nothing. (*He takes a letter from his trouser pocket*) I forgot to tell you, this came this morning. (*He throws it on the bench and moves away down* L)
Shirley What is it?
Gareth It's a letter.
Shirley From who?
Gareth Parkinson Fryer.
Shirley Your works?

He nods

What does it say?
Gareth Read it.
Shirley No, tell me.
Gareth It's my notice. I've been made redundant.
Shirley Redundant? That's a bit sudden isn't it? It's not fair to spring it on you like that.
Gareth There was a lot of talk about it a couple of weeks ago. I didn't tell you about it because I didn't want you to worry. I know how important my job is to you.
Shirley What's that supposed to mean?
Gareth Well it is isn't it? I mean it's no fun being on the dole, ask Ken.
Shirley Ken's not on the dole now, he's got a job.

Gareth Course he has. (*He moves to go inside*) Silly bloody me. How could I forget that.

Shirley Where are you going?

Gareth (*at the door*) I don't know. Out!

Shirley Where?

Gareth Anywhere!

Shirley (*after a slight pause*) Don't go? Stay here with me. Talk to me out here while everyone's in there eating.

There is a pause

Come on. We don't get the chance to be alone very often. Let's make the most of it.

Gareth (*turning slightly*) What do you want to say?

Shirley I don't want to say anything in particular. I just want to talk. Make plans.

Gareth (*facing her*) With no job?

Shirley We can dream, can't we?

Gareth (*after a pause*) Come and sit down. (*He leads her to sit on the deckchair. He wanders around the garden*)

There is a pause

Shirley Perhaps it's not such a bad thing.

He looks at her

Your redundancy.

Gareth You're not serious?

Shirley They'll pay you up, won't they?

Gareth They're going to pay me sod all.

Shirley You're bound to have something, surely.

Gareth I haven't been there long enough. You don't get anything for the first two years.

Shirley No lump sum then.

Gareth Might be able to afford a cot; a second-hand pram, and a couple of things for the baby. If we're lucky we might be able to paper the bedroom. Not much of a start in life for it, is it?

Shirley I wonder what it'll be, a boy or a girl. What would you like?

Gareth I don't care much.

They look at each other

As long as everything is all right.

She smiles

You still want to have the baby here, then?

Shirley (*panicking slightly*) I don't want to go to hospital.

Gareth No OK. OK. (*He pauses*) Perhaps, when I get another job, and when I've saved enough, we'll have a place of our own and get out of this house once and for all.

There is a pause

Well, say something.

Shirley Like what?

Gareth Agree with me. You want a place of your own, don't you?

Shirley Doesn't every girl?

Gareth So why the silence?

Shirley I was just thinking, that's all. About where we'd live. They're putting up some lovely houses down on the common. They won't be ready until next March.

Gareth I wouldn't have saved enough by then. (*He goes and kneels on the grass to her right*) I'd like you to have one, though. I'd like you to have what you want.

Shirley I can see us in one of *them*.

Gareth I can try, but I can't make any promises.

Shirley That's good enough for me.

Gareth So you'd leave here then?

Shirley What do you mean? Of course I would.

Gareth (*smiling*) Down on the common. All the snobs live there.

Shirley I don't care. (*She jerks sharply*)

Gareth What's the matter?

Shirley He kicked me that's all. Give me your hand. (*She takes his hand and puts it on her stomach*) Can you feel it?

Gareth (*waiting then smiling*) Yeah, it's moving.

Shirley Of course it is.

He looks at her and she smiles at him. This is probably the closest they've been in some time. He gets up on to his knees and is about to kiss her when...

Mrs Morris comes to the garden wall

Mrs Morris Gareth? (*She sees them close together*)

They spring apart

Oh, what's the matter?

Gareth (*improvising*) Er ... it's Shirley. She's got something in her eye.

Mrs Morris A fly I expect—they're everywhere. (*Waving her hand in the air as she speaks*) Is your mother there?

Gareth Yes.

Mrs Morris Well could you give her a shout for me?

Gareth (*calling*) Mam!

There is no answer

Mam!

Doris (*off*) What do you want?

Gareth What's-her-name wants you.

Doris (*off*) Who?

Gareth What-you-call-it.

Doris appears at the back door

Doris Who the hell is what-you-call-it?

Mrs Morris Me. It's me, Doris.

Doris (*coming into the garden*) Oh, Audrey. (*To Gareth*) Why didn't you say. (*She clips him across the head as she passes behind him*)
Gareth I did.

Gareth goes off into the house. Shirley follows after him

Mrs Morris I was going to say that I've just come back from the chemist. I had to go there to get some calamine lotion for my rash—and Will Pickett wasn't there.
Doris Well that's not unusual, he's never there until five o'clock to give out the prescriptions.
Mrs Morris Yes I know. But me pleading ignorant, I said to the girl behind the counter, "Mr Pickett there please?" I said. And do you know what she told me?
Doris No.
Mrs Morris He's gone away. "Gone away," I said. "That's a bit funny, 'cause I saw him last night"—and then she told me.
Doris What?
Mrs Morris That he flew this morning to Torremolinos. Well, that's a bit strange, I said, 'cause only last week he was telling me that he wouldn't be having a holiday this year on account of the business. There was no mention of Torremolinos then.
Doris So you think he's gone on the strength of Auntie Alice's will?
Mrs Morris Well your guess is as good as mine.
Doris Oh Arthur will be furious.
Mrs Morris I've been trying to put a few feelers out to see how much she's left—but no-one seems to know anything about it.
Doris It won't take long. News like that spreads like a forest fire.

Kenneth comes out of the house wearing dark glasses

Kenneth Any aspirin here or something. I've got a headache.
Doris They're in the sideboard.
Kenneth No they're not, I've looked.
Doris Well ask your father then, he had them last.
Kenneth I have. He said he hasn't seen them.
Doris He has. He's the only one who ever uses them. He'll take an aspirin for anything that man.
Mrs Morris Fred's the same. We've got something to do, with all of them.

Doris and Mrs Morris ad-lib their moans and groans about their husbands. Kenneth interrupts them when he clears his throat. Doris looks around not expecting to see him there

Kenneth Eh, hum!
Doris I suppose you want me to have a look for them now, do you?
Kenneth Yeah. If you would.
Doris (*to Mrs Morris*) See you later.

She goes off into the house

Kenneth is about to follow her, but . . .

Mrs Morris How are you then, Ken? Still not working.

Kenneth stops. His back is to Mrs Morris. He decides that this is a perfect opportunity to send her up

Kenneth No. I start on Monday though.

Mrs Morris Oh, what doing?

Kenneth (*going to the garden wall*) Canvassing. I'm going round the doors selling contraceptives.

She looks amazed

Can I interest you in any?

Mrs Morris Are you serious?

Kenneth All sales are confidential. I've signed an oath not to name anybody, or write a book about it if and when I should finish—or get the sack of course, which ever should come first.

Mrs Morris People don't buy those now, they're on the National Health.

Kenneth Ah, yes. The National Health ones are on the National Health. But you can't get the ones *I* sell on prescription.

Mrs Morris Why's that?

Kenneth Because they've got a side effect.

Mrs Morris Oh well they're no good then are they if they've got a side effect.

Kenneth But that's what I'm selling. I'm not selling the pill—I'm selling the side effect.

Mrs Morris What *is* the side effect?

After checking that they are alone in the garden he leans closer to her

Kenneth A guaranteed ten-minute orgasm.

Mrs Morris (*screaming*) Ten minutes?

He nods

Go on, you're having me on.

Kenneth No it's right enough.

Mrs Morris is elated at the possibility. Kenneth turns away to laugh, he can't keep a straight face any longer. Suddenly Mrs Morris has thought of a hitch

Mrs Morris Hey, listen—what if you can't stand for it to last ten minutes?

Kenneth (*turning to face her he improvises madly*) Ah, well, then you take another pill, called Curtailier Pleasuritis—that's it's correct name—and then Bob's your uncle. (*He snaps his fingers*)

By this time Mrs Morris is completely taken in

Mrs Morris Curtailier Pleasuritis.

Kenneth nods, leading her on

I've got to go in for a minute. I think Fred's calling me. What's the name of those pills again?

Kenneth tells her. She repeats the name over and over as she goes in

Fred ...

Mrs Morris goes into her house

Kenneth (*laughing heartily; in Mrs Morris' voice*) Fred, I've decided what I want for my birthday. (*Still laughing he collapses on the grass trying to pull himself together*)

Shirley comes out of the kitchen eating an apple

Shirley Oh. You're out here are you.
Kenneth (*attempting to get up*) Yeah, come and lie down.
Shirley (*going to the bench*) No I'd better not. I have trouble getting up.
Kenneth Yeah, you're getting a big girl now.
Shirley That's because I eat all my dinner. Which is more than I can say for you.
Kenneth I'm fed up with salad. If I eat any more I'll swear I'll turn into a bloody lettuce. (*After a slight pause*) I'm off my food anyway.
Shirley Why's that?
Kenneth Well, I haven't been the same since you told me about ... the baby.
Shirley Shock too much for you was it?
Kenneth It's not that ... it's just that I feel ... well, ill all the time.
Shirley Ill?
Kenneth Yes. Especially in the mornings. I get as sick as a dog.

She laughs

You can laugh, but it's true—I get sympathy pains.
Shirley You're all right, are you?
Kenneth I do. I can't sleep some nights with an aching in my back, and it's only since you told me about the baby.
Shirley It's all in the mind.
Kenneth I wish it was. I took this book out of the library, and a Professor Kingsley or someone said, that it is possible for some fathers to feel the pains of pregnancy, especially if the parents to-be are extremely close.
Shirley That's providing you are the father.
Kenneth I am, Shirl. I know I am.
Shirley How?
Kenneth Because of the way I feel. I've never felt this way before.
Shirley You sound as though you're going to break into song any minute.
Kenneth You can joke about it but I know I am the father.
Shirley What do you think you are? Some kind of prophet? A clairvoyant? Nobody knows who the father is. Not even me.

Gareth comes into the garden

Gareth Shirley, Dad wants to know—(*he pauses as he sees them together*)—if you're ready for your dinner.
Shirley No, I'll have mine later when you've all gone out.
Gareth (*standing* R *of Kenneth*) Those are my glasses, aren't they? (*Indicating the sunglasses Kenneth is wearing*)
Kenneth Are they?

Gareth Yeah, where did you have them from?

Kenneth Behind the photo on the sideboard. (*He stands*)

Gareth Yeah, they're mine. I put them there one day last week.

Kenneth takes them off and hands them to him. Gareth goes to take them but changes his mind. Kenneth puts them back on and moves slightly down L

Doris comes out with the aspirin

Doris Here you are, Kenneth. You couldn't have looked very far—I put my hands on them straight away. (*She gives the bottle to Kenneth*) You'd better take a couple now or you'll have a headache all through the funeral.

Kenneth I don't think I'll go.

Gareth looks at him

Doris Why?

Kenneth (*half-looking towards Shirley*) I think I'd better stay home.

Gareth looks at Shirley. She is looking at Kenneth

Doris There's no need to stay home. If you take two now you'll be all right by one o'clock.

Kenneth (*going into the house*) No. No I'm not going.

He exits

Doris (*following Kenneth*) Well what the hell's got into him.

She exits

Gareth (*after Doris has gone*) Why has he changed his mind?

Shirley I don't know. Because he's got a headache I suppose.

Gareth Will you change your mind?

Shirley About what?

Gareth The funeral.

At this point Mrs Morris comes to the garden wall. She has been rushing. The following dialogue should be fast with no gaps

Shirley No, I told you, I can't.

Mrs Morris Where's Kenneth?

Gareth Please?

Shirley No, not looking like this.

Mrs Morris In the house, is he?

Gareth I want you to come with me.

Shirley You'll only be gone a couple of hours.

Gareth That's long enough.

Shirley For what?

Mrs Morris Give him a shout for me will you, Gareth?

Gareth Please come with me, Shirley, please?

Shirley I don't know why you're making all this fuss. Why is it so important?

Mrs Morris Fred wants a word with him.

Gareth Because it *is* important.
Shirley Why!
Gareth (*raising his voice*) Because otherwise you'll be here with him.
Shirley (*standing as she shouts*) With who?
Gareth (*still shouting*) Ken!
Mrs Morris He won't keep him long.

Shirley goes off into the house

Oh, was it something I said?
Gareth Shit!
Mrs Morris Pardon?
Gareth (*shouting at Mrs Morris*) I said shit! Shit! Shit! Shit!

He turns and goes into the house shouting

Mrs Morris (*calling after him*) Tell Kenneth I want him. Tell him Fred
wants him. Tell him to call round. Gareth? Gareth! Gareth.

Her last "Gareth" tails off as the Lights dim to a Black-out

SCENE 2

The same. Later the same afternoon

*The Lights come up on Shirley who is sitting in the deck-chair, reading the
newspaper and eating a box of chocolates*

Mrs Morris comes into her garden to check on her washing. She spots Shirley

Mrs Morris (*at the wall*) Another warm one.
Shirley (*after looking around*) Pardon?
Mrs Morris I said it's another warm one.
Shirley What is?
Mrs Morris The weather. The weather's hot.
Shirley Oh, yes. (*She returns to her newspaper*)
Mrs Morris Anything interesting?

Shirley looks up. She doesn't want to be bothered. She looks over to her

In the paper?
Shirley No, not really.
Mrs Morris Hey, did you read about that woman last week?
Shirley (*without looking up*) What woman?
Mrs Morris She was having a baby by her husband three years after he was
dead.
Shirley Impossible.
Mrs Morris I said that as well, but it's right enough. It said something
about they deep-freezed it. Kept it in a sperm bank. I said to Fred, I said,
"It's a wonder Barclays haven't thought of that," I said. Still, it was
interesting reading though. Told you all about it from beginning to end.

Shirley (*a little more interested*) Even how she conceived?

Mrs Morris Oh yes. It told you all about that. Told you all about the artificial insemination. It's marvellous what they can do today, isn't it? Especially where sex is concerned—it's a pill for this and a pill for—that reminds me, I knew there was something I wanted—is Kenneth there?

Shirley I don't think he's come back yet.

Mrs Morris Course he's gone to the funeral hasn't he?

Shirley No, he didn't go after. He had a headache. He went out for a walk about half an hour ago.

Mrs Morris Oh, I'll see him when he comes back then. Well, it's Fred that wants to see him not me. (*After a pause*) I'm glad he's got a job.

Shirley looks at her

Kenneth. He hasn't had the best of luck between everything, has he?

Shirley smiles, not really wanting to smile at all. There is a pause

How's your mother, Shirley, I haven't seen her for ages.

Shirley She's all right.

Mrs Morris And your father?

Shirley nods

Good. He gets about all right, don't he, with that wooden thing he's got?

Shirley You mean his artificial leg?

Mrs Morris Yes. I saw him running for a bus one day last week. Never thought I'd see the day. Running full pelt down Argate Street he was.

Shirley Dad? Running for a bus.

Mrs Morris Yes, I couldn't get over it. Course he missed it mind, but that's not the point is it? I said to Fred, I said "That's not the point," I said. "It's a miracle that man can stand", I said, "let alone run for a bus."

Doris (*off, from inside the house*) Shirley. Shirley where are you?

Shirley (*calling*) I'm out here.

Doris comes out into the garden

Doris Oh, do me a favour. Go and pour me a glass of squash will you? I'm parched. (*To Mrs Morris*) I'm just about cooking in this dress.

Mrs Morris I was just saying it's a warm one.

Shirley struggles to get out of the deck-chair

Shirley (*to Doris*) Can you give me a hand!

Doris Yes all right. (*She goes to the back of the deck-chair and yanks her out from behind*)

Shirley goes into the house

Doris moves back to Mrs Morris

Mrs Morris Nice funeral?

Doris Lovely.

Mrs Morris Ham or beef?

Doris (*as if ham isn't good enough*) Beef. She had a beautiful service. He said some nice things about her. None of them were true mind—but he said some nice things. He was going on about how the family was going to miss her, and what good she'd done for charity—I thought I was in the wrong funeral for a minute. Oh, if I don't get out of this dress soon, I'll choke.

Mrs Morris It's nice though. Black suits you.

Doris beams

And it fits you almost everywhere.

Doris You could swear I'd asked Shirley to fetch that squash from her mother's, the time she's taking.

Mrs Morris You can't rush in this weather though, can you?

Doris She's the same in any weather. She can't help it I know, but I feel like giving her a good shaking sometimes. Only yesterday I told her to go and peg some clothes out, and by the time she got round to it they'd dried in the basket. I'm not being funny but she's too slow to catch a ...

Shirley comes out carrying a glass of squash

She is seen first by Mrs Morris who tries without saying anything to tell Doris she is coming behind her. Doris gets the message and turns

They laugh

Oh thank you Shirley love. (*She drinks it down in one*)

Shirley makes for the bench

Oh, I needed that. Weak it was, though. I like my squash a bit stronger than that.

Shirley reacts

Shirley (*sitting*) Didn't Gareth come home the same time as you?

Doris No, he left the funeral ages before us. Didn't he come back here?

Shirley I haven't seen him.

Doris looks at Mrs Morris, then at Shirley

Doris You and him are all right, are you?

Shirley Yes.

Doris Had a bit of a tiff, have you?

Mrs Morris nods, and mouths that she witnessed it

Shirley No, not really. He wanted me to go with him to the funeral, that's all.

Doris (*to Mrs Morris*) I don't know what's the matter with our Gareth lately. Pick, pick, pick that's all he's doing—and our Ken can't even look at him. He's at his throat for the least little thing.

Mrs Morris It's a wonder for Gareth too, he's usually the nicer of the two.

Doris looks at her

(*Realizing what she has said*) Well you know what I mean, not nicer, that's the wrong word. I didn't mean that Ken *wasn't* nice. I didn't mean that at all. What I meant was that, well Gareth's more pleasant, isn't he? (*She's done it again*) No not pleasant—he's *not* pleasant, well I mean he *is* pleasant. Your Gareth *is* pleasant. And Kenneth—Kenneth's pleasant too. What I meant to say was that, well Gareth's more . . . you know . . . more, what's the word now . . . more . . . um . . . I'm going to have to go in, I've got migraine coming.

She disappears into her house

Doris (*after a pause*) I'm sure she's on the change. (*She comes to sit on the bench next to Shirley*) Are you sure there's nothing wrong between you and Gareth?
Shirley No, nothing.

Doris looks at her suspiciously

Doris There is something, I'm sure.

Pause. Shirley looks away impatiently. Another pause

Well, are you going to tell me whose fault it is or am I going to have to ask Gareth?
Shirley It's nobody's fault. I told you, he wanted me to go to the funeral with him and I wouldn't.
Doris That's all? That's all it's over?
Shirley (*nodding*) I know why he's a bit irritable today, though. (*After a slight pause*) He's been made redundant.
Doris Redundant?

Shirley nods

Our Gareth.
Shirley Yes.
Doris He hasn't said a word to me.
Shirley Ask him to show you the letter if you don't believe me.
Doris I will when he comes in.

Kenneth comes into the garden carrying a large cardboard box

Kenneth You're all back then?
Doris All except Gareth. You haven't seen him, I suppose?
Kenneth No. How did it go?
Doris All right. Arthur made a fool of himself but that's nothing unusual. Where've you been?
Kenneth I went out.
Doris I gathered that.
Kenneth Shirley wanted me to run an errand. (*To Shirley*) They didn't have any in Pickett's or Boots either.
Doris What was it you were after?
Kenneth Hairgrips.

Doris (*incredulously*) Hairgrips. There's two packets of hairgrips in the front room.

Kenneth Shirley wanted white ones.

Doris They are white. I won't use them. (*To Shirley*) I told you yesterday you could have them, Shirley.

Shirley (*embarrassed*) I must have forgotten.

Kenneth and Shirley look at each other. Kenneth realizes he was sent on a fool's errand. Doris breaks the stare

Doris (*pointing to the cardboard box*) What have you got there?

Kenneth (*hurt*) It's er ... it's a present—for the baby.

Doris For the baby? It's not due till September.

Kenneth Well, never mind. (*He hands it to Shirley*)

Doris What is it?

Kenneth (*to Shirley*) Open it.

She does and takes out an enormous panda

Shirley (*embarrassed*) You shouldn't have.

Doris What did you want to go and waste your money on a thing like that for?

Kenneth It's my money.

Doris It's too big. It's too big for a baby.

Kenneth He'll grow won't he?

Doris Grow? He'll have to have lessons with a bloody bullworker to handle that thing. (*She goes into the house speaking as she goes*) You're going off your head, you are. Reg, come and see what this boy has bought, he's going soft in the head.

Doris exits

There is a pause

Kenneth Do you like it?

Shirley It's lovely.

Kenneth You don't seem very pleased.

Shirley I said it's lovely.

Kenneth I'll change it for something else if you'd rather.

Shirley No. (*Quietly*) It's lovely.

There is another pause. She puts the toy to sit on the bench

Kenneth You did it on purpose, didn't you?

She can't answer him

Two packets in the front room. (*After a slight pause*) I must have gone to every chemist from here to flaming Ashton. (*The name of any local town may be used. After a slight pause*) Why?

She doesn't answer

Why didn't you just tell me to bugger off.

Shirley Would you have?

Kenneth (*after thinking about it*) Probably not. (*After a pause*) Why did you do it to me?

Shirley I didn't do it to you—I did it to myself. I couldn't bear to be in the same room as you.

Kenneth Do you hate me that much?

Shirley Oh Ken!

He moves towards her

No, don't touch me.

A pause

Kenneth I wanted to rush back—to be here before the others. Then I had the idea to buy something for the baby. It couldn't be any old thing—it had to be special. (*After a slight pause*) I got carried away. Time just flew.

Shirley We've got to let go, Ken.

Kenneth We?

Shirley I mean *you*.

Kenneth (*after a slight pause*) Why do you always fight me?

Shirley We don't fight we ... (*She almost says "flirt"*)

Kenneth Go on. Say it.

Pause

Say it?

Shirley (*almost crying*) I can't.

Kenneth You have a clever way of keeping the fire burning, Shirley.

Shirley Only because I don't know how to put it out—for good.

Kenneth Answer me honestly. If you could, would you? Put me out, I mean.

Shirley (*becoming upset*) Of course I would. You don't think I enjoy feeling like this, do you?

Kenneth Feeling like what?

She realizes what she has said

Tell me. Admit you feel something. (*He goes to her*) Don't fight me.

Shirley If I don't I'll give in. And I can't do that. I can't.

Kenneth (*embracing her*) Don't cry. (*Wiping away her tears with his thumb*) Don't cry don't cry.

Shirley (*breaking down completely*) I can't go on much longer, Ken. Living in this house with you – with Gareth the way he is. I don't know where I am. And I'm all mixed up and I'm hot ... I'm hot. (*She breaks away from him. After a slight pause*) Gareth knows, I'm sure he does.

Kenneth Has he said anything?

Shirley Does he have to? You know what he's like to you. To everyone.

Kenneth (*after quickly thinking it over*) No. No he'd have said something. He'd never be able to keep something like that to himself.

Shirley Then why is he like he is?

He shrugs

And you don't help either.

Kenneth What do you mean?

Shirley Not going to the funeral. You should have gone, Ken—you should have. He told me he didn't want me to be here with you.

Kenneth Did he?

Shirley He didn't want us to be alone together.

There is a pause. He looks at her

Kenneth So what do we do now?

Shirley (*crying again*) I don't know.

Suddenly Gareth is heard shouting from inside the house

Gareth (*off*) I don't care. I just don't bloody care!

Doris (*also off*) I'm not having you coming in this house in that state in the afternoon.

Kenneth and Shirley look at each other

I'm not having it. I'm not having it, Reg.

Kenneth looks towards the house and takes one or two steps nearer

I'm warning you, Gareth, you can cut it out when you like. It's not fair. It's not fair, Reg.

Reg (*off*) Tell him not me.

Doris (*off*) It's not fair and I'm not having it.

Gareth steps out into the garden

Gareth Oh bollocks! (*He sees Shirley and Kenneth*) Well well, if it isn't Mr and Mrs Price.

Kenneth You're drunk.

Gareth Something you've never been I suppose?

Doris comes to stand in the kitchen doorway. She watches. Grandad looks on through the kitchen blinds

Yeah, I'm drunk and isn't it awful? Isn't it terrible? Drunk in the afternoon—and he's on the dole too, with a wife to support and a baby on the way.

Kenneth turns to look at Shirley

(*Addressing Kenneth*) Isn't it shameful? Well, isn't it? (*He doesn't have Kenneth's attention. He pushes him hard on his shoulder*) Isn't it? (*Suddenly he spots the panda on the bench*) What the hell's that?·

Shirley is reluctant to answer. She knows it will aggravate the situation. Eventually the silence forces her to

Shirley It's a panda.

Gareth What's it doing here?

Shirley Ken bought it.

Gareth Ken?

Shirley For the baby.

Gareth (*shouting*) Nobody buys nothing for my baby, do you hear? Not my baby. (*To Kenneth*) *Me*, I buy everything that kid needs. Understand? You don't buy that baby nothing. (*He pushes him on the shoulder again*) Nothing!

Gareth pushes him on the shoulder again, harder this time and Kenneth begins to push him back. Within seconds they are punching each other. They are not fighting for too long though before Doris parts them

Doris Come on—get in that house.

Kenneth stops fighting but his eyes are fixed firmly on Gareth

In that house, I said.

Doris grabs him by the shoulder of his shirt and forces him into the house. Kenneth has the last word though before he goes

Kenneth (*shouting at Gareth*) You silly sod!

Doris and Kenneth exit

Gareth (*shouting back*) Yes, aren't I?

There is a pause. After some time he turns to Shirley

Am I?
Shirley (*quietly*) What?
Gareth A silly sod?
Shirley (*moving to him*) Come on, let's go in.
Gareth (*still shouting*) I don't want to go in yet. You go in if you want to.
Shirley (*moving a little nearer*) Don't make a scene. Someone might see you out here.
Gareth (*facing her, pointing to her with his left hand*) You'll want me one day. One day you'll call me and I won't come. (*He pauses*) You'd better go in. Go on, go in.

Shirley moves closer to him and touches his arm. He flings it away with his

No, I'm all right. Go in. I want you to.
Shirley Look, I know we haven't been very good lately.
Gareth That's a laugh.
Shirley But you don't know what it's like for *me*.
Gareth Oh a right bloody martyr.
Shirley (*crying again*) It's not easy living in that house, you know.
Gareth Go inside.
Shirley And you're nasty sometimes.
Gareth (*raising his voice*) Go inside.
Shirley Nasty for no reason at all.
Gareth (*shouting as he points to the house with his right arm extended*) Get in that bloody house!

By this time, Shirley is an emotional wreck. She rushes off into the house

There is a long pause while Gareth pulls himself together a little. He sits on the bench, head in his hands. After a time he looks up. He senses someone is looking at him. He turns slightly and sees the panda. He sits back on the bench and speaks

What did you think of that then, eh? Did I exercise my authority as a married man? Did I put my foot down with a firm hand? Did I? (*After a slight pause*) It's not going to make any difference anyway, is it? And I don't like rows. In fact I hate rows. But what else can I do, only make rows? What would you do? Oh I know what you'd do but I can't do that. You understand though, don't you? You understand my position. I mean you can see what sort of spot I'm in? (*He laughs*) Spot! Get it? (*Pointing to the panda's eye*) That's a funny word for it, isn't it? (*He laughs again but the laugh gradually turns to tears*) I wish I was a bloody panda.

The Lights dim to a Black-out

ACT III

SCENE 1

The same. 7.45 pm on a warm late September night

The CURTAIN *comes up on an empty stage. After a few seconds the toilet flushes and Grandad comes out. He crosses to the deck-chair. After quickly checking to see that no-one is about, he takes a small bottle of gin from his inside pocket and drinks about half the contents. He manages to put the bottle back into his pocket and sit in the deck-chair before . . .*

Shirley comes out from the house, carrying a teapot which she empties down the drain. She is about to go back into the house when . . .

Grandad (*calling*) Shirley?

Shirley Yes, Grandad?

Grandad Have you got a minute?

Shirley (*going to him*) Course I have. What do you want?

Grandad Just a little chat that's all. Nothing very much.

Shirley Something bothering? (*Going to the bench*)

Grandad Well I don't know.

Shirley (*sitting*) What is it?

Grandad (*after a pause*) I know I'm old —and I get confused, I know that too. But I can't seem to make head nor tail of it somehow.

Shirley Of what?

Grandad Well, let me start from the beginning. You are married, aren't you?

Shirley Yes.

Grandad Now, I'm right up to there. This is where I go wrong now. And you're married to . . . (*He thinks very carefully for a moment*) Kenneth.

Shirley No, Gareth.

Grandad See what I mean? I get confused. One day I think it's Ken you're married to and the next I think it's Gareth.

Shirley Well it's Gareth I'm married to, you can take it from me.

Grandad Not Kenneth?

Shirley Gareth.

Grandad (*happy that he's got it straight*) Gareth.

Doris comes out of the house

Doris Any hopes of that teapot, or are we going to have to drink coffee instead?

Shirley (*standing*) I'm just coming.

She goes into the house

Grandad (*after Shirley has gone*) Doris.
Doris What?
Grandad (*proud that he's finally cracked it*) It's Gareth she's married to then . . .
Doris Well who the hell do you think she's married to?
Grandad I don't know. I wonder sometimes.

Doris is about to go back into the house when she stops and begins to sniff the air. Grandad looks at her and begins to do the same

Doris There's a strong smell of drink out here.
Grandad Now it's funny you should say that because I'm sure that Shirley's on the gin.

Doris gives him a disbelieving look as she attempts once more to go into the house

Mrs Morris comes to the garden wall and calls her

Mrs Morris Yoo hoo! (*To Doris*) You haven't got .two fifty-pence pieces? Our light has just gone out.
Doris I haven't, I know. Have you, Dad?
Grandad What?
Doris Got two fifty-pence pieces for Audrey?
Grandad I'll have a look.
Doris He might have some.
Mrs Morris Ta.

Grandad stands and takes out a small purse. As he opens it, Doris peeps over his shoulder to see how much cash he is carrying. He sees her and turns away

Doris Your washing has dried lovely.
Mrs Morris Yes. It's been a nice day though, hasn't it. I'll have to take it in later.
Grandad (*going to the garden fence*) Two you wanted?
Mrs Morris Well, one will do if you've got it.
Grandad No, no. I've got two. (*He hands her the money and peers down her cleavage*) Nice day.
Mrs Morris (*exchanging the money*) Thank you, that's lovely.

Doris sees what he's up to and calls him

Doris Hey! There's a cup of tea on the table if you want it.
Grandad Yes, I'm just going in. (*To Mrs Morris*) I'll see you again. (*He salutes Doris as he passes her*)

He exits into the house

Mrs Morris No news yet then, with Shirley.
Doris (*moving to the wall*) No, nothing.

Mrs Morris Hanging on well, isn't she?
Doris More than a week overdue.
Mrs Morris Anytime now then?
Doris Yes. I've got everything prepared though, so we're all ready.

There is a pause

Mrs Morris (*after a thought*) Hey, your Arthur got off lucky then.
Doris Yes. He thought he would have had jail.
Mrs Morris He should never have gone to meet Will Pickett at the airport.
Doris Shoot first and ask questions after – that's our Arthur.
Mrs Morris And to hit him twice – in front of all those people.
Doris He'd only just come through Customs.
Mrs Morris (*shaking her head*) And all because of a nasty old rumour.
Doris Fancy somebody spreading things like that about.
Mrs Morris I mean there's no point in it, is there?
Doris Some horrible people living around here.
Mrs Morris I've always said it. I've always said it about the people round
here. Well, there's one thing, Doris, our consciences are clear.

At this point Kenneth rushes out of the house and straight into the toilet. He
makes a noise as he goes

What was that?
Doris Our Ken. (*She speaks a little quiet*) There's something wrong with
him, I'm sure. He's trying not to show it but there's *something* wrong with
him.
Mrs Morris What is it, do you think?
Doris I don't know. I don't know what it is but he can't sit still for two
minutes. And he's in and out of the toilet all the time.
Mrs Morris There's a lot of dysentery about.
Doris No, it's not that. It's not dysentery. He's been sick too, I think.
Mrs Morris Sick?

Doris nods

I wonder what's the matter with him.
Doris I can't quite put my finger on it.

Shirley comes into the garden

Shirley The cot's come.
Doris (*to Mrs Morris*) I'd better go in. I'll see you again.

Doris goes inside

Shirley is about to follow her, but …

Mrs Morris How're you feeling, Shirley?
Shirley (*turning to face her*) Big!!
Mrs Morris Never mind, won't be long now.
Shirley (*going to her*) It's elephants I feel sorry for.
Mrs Morris Elephants?

Shirley They carry for nearly two years.

Mrs Morris (*amazed*) Do they? (*After a slight pause*) Hey, I bet you have a problem finding things to fit you now.

Shirley If I get any bigger I'll have to go around naked.

Mrs Morris (*taking her seriously*) Oh you can't do that. You won't be able to go out anywhere.

Shirley (*sending her up*) Oh I will, in the night, when it gets dark.

Mrs Morris Dark? Dark! Oh hell, I'd better go in—I've forgotten about Fred, he's sitting there with no light on. I'll see you, Shirley.

She rushes off

Shirley wanders down to the bench

The toilet flushes and Kenneth comes out. He is in a bit of a state. He sees Shirley

Kenneth (*going towards her*) Hey, are you feeling all right?

Shirley Yes why?

Kenneth (*hands on stomach*) Oh I feel terrible.

Shirley I can't see how you say you get sympathy pains if I don't get them as well.

Kenneth Well I do and I've got a bad stomach to prove it.

Shirley Well I feel all——(*She jerks with a pain in her stomach*)

Kenneth does as well

Kenneth (*after the pain*) What was that then?

Shirley (*trying not to show*) Nothing.

Kenneth You had a pain then, didn't you?

Shirley It wasn't very much.

Kenneth But you had one, didn't you?

Shirley (*reluctantly*) Yes. (*She looks at him*)

Kenneth And me.

Shirley It doesn't mean anything.

Kenneth I get one every twenty minutes, I've timed them.

Shirley Are you sure?

Kenneth (*checking his watch*) Yes. Only that last one wasn't a twenty-minute one. It was a five-minute one.

Shirley (*more concerned now*) You don't think it's labour, do you?

Kenneth I don't know. I think it might be.

She takes Kenneth's arm and leads him to the bench

Shirley Well let's sit down and wait for another one. (*She sits him down then sits herself*)

Kenneth (*rubbing his back*) I haven't been right all day. And I've had niggly pains in my back all afternoon.

Shirley That's a sure sign.

Kenneth I'll be glad when it's all over. Perhaps I'll get a decent night's sleep then.

Shirley *I* sleep all right.

Kenneth That's what doesn't seem fair. You've gone through it all like a bull.

Shirley looks at him

Well, not a *bull*.

Shirley A cow?

Kenneth No. You know what I mean. And there's me I've been as sick as a dog from the start.

They both jerk with pain

You too?

Shirley Yes. They're getting quicker, aren't they?

Before he can answer, Reg and Gareth come out of the house carrying a baby's cot which needs to be assembled

Doris (*off, shouting to them as they leave the house*) Yes, put it up out there—there's no room for you to do it in here.

Reg (*putting it down on the ground, down R*) Here will do.

Shirley Putting the cot up, are you?

Gareth May as well—there's nothing on the telly.

Author's note: Reg and Gareth's dialogue in the following scene can be adapted to fit in with the construction of the cot. The cot is assembled on-stage and the dialogue fitted in as necessary. You may also need to take some of the dialogue out in order that the completion of the cot be exercised as smoothly as possible

Gareth moves the deck-chair so that they have more room for the cot

Reg Where's the plans? There are supposed to be plans here somewhere.

Shirley They're usually in a little plastic bag.

Reg (*finding them*) Oh yes, here they are.

Reg takes out the plans and looks at them. Gareth spreads all parts of the cot on to the grass

That's all, is it?

Shirley Is there anything missing?

Gareth No, everything's here, I think.

Shirley It doesn't look very much when it's all out, does it?

Shirley and Kenneth shriek simultaneously with pain

Gareth (*to Shirley*) What's the matter?

Shirley Nothing. It looks nice with that transfer, doesn't it?

Gareth continues to set out the cot on the ground while Shirley looks at Kenneth apprehensively and Kenneth nods to confirm

Reg (*reading the instructions aloud*) "Take part A and connect with part B." Have you got that, Gareth?

Gareth (*picking up the head of the cot*) Well, this is part A, (*taking the side of the cot*) and this is part B.

Reg Well, fix them together then.

Gareth tries to connect the two parts

Shirley (*trying to make conversation*) Shall I fetch the mattress?
Reg No, we won't be needing that yet, Shirley love.
Gareth These don't fit together.
Reg You've got the right parts, have you? A and B.
Gareth Yes. (*He looks at the instructions that Reg is holding*) Let me see.
   That's right, yeah.

Reg takes the instructions again

Reg Well, that's what it says. "Fix A to B". Oh, "by inserting part C."
   That's this bracket here.

Gareth takes the bracket and connects the parts

Shirley Can I give you a——

Shirley and Kenneth shriek together again

Gareth (*to Shirley*) Are you sure you're all right?
Shirley Of course I am. I had a little pain, that's all.
Gareth Where?
Shirley It's all right. It's not time yet.
Reg Are you sure, Shirley? Perhaps you'd better go and lay down.
Gareth Yeah you're looking a bit flushed. (*Calling*) Mam? Mam!
Doris (*off, from inside the house*) What do you want? I'm watching
   television.
Gareth Come here, it's Shirley.
Shirley I'm all right.

   Doris appears at the back door

Doris I've told you before not to bother me when I'm watching telly. What
   do you want?
Gareth It's Shirley. She's not very well.
Shirley (*insisting*) I'm all right.
Gareth She's had a pain.
Shirley It was nothing.
Doris (*going to Shirley*) You haven't started?
Shirley I don't know. I don't think so.
Doris You'd better come upstairs with me.
Shirley It was hardly anything. It was probably that kipper I had for tea.
Doris (*looking at Shirley in amazement*) Kipper? (*She takes her by the arm*)
   Upstairs!

   They both go inside

Gareth Do you think the baby is on its way?
Reg I don't know—but we'd better get on with this just in case.
Gareth Come on then.
Reg Now—(*reading the instructions*)—"put part D next to part E and
   secure with F." (*Looking around the floor*) Where's F?

Gareth It's that bottom part there, I think.

Reg picks up the part and fixes it to the now fast-appearing frame

Mrs Morris appears at the garden wall

Mrs Morris Yoo hoo, it's me again. Oh it's you, Ken. Is your mother there?
Kenneth (*still very uncomfortable*) She's upstairs.
Mrs Morris Well it's her father I wanted really. I asked him a few minutes
ago for two fifty-pence pieces.

Kenneth moves to the wall

He gave me them but I could only get one in the meter. (*Showing the coin
to Kenneth*) This is a foreign one, look.
Kenneth (*taking a coin from his pocket*) You'd better have this one instead
then. (*As he gives it to her he pulls a face and puts a hand on his stomach*)
Mrs Morris Ta. What's the matter?
Kenneth Nothing.
Mrs Morris What did you make that face for then?
Kenneth I've got a bad stomach.
Mrs Morris I've got some Settlers in the house if you want them.

He shakes his head

Upstairs you said your mother is?
Kenneth Yes, with Shirley.
Mrs Morris (*excited*) She hasn't started?
Kenneth Well I don't know. (*He has another pain*) I think she might have,
yes.
Mrs Morris Oh, I'll go and tell Fred. (*She rushes off*) Better check that
there's petrol in the car. You never know, she might change her mind.
And don't forget—if you want those Settlers—give me a knock.

She goes

*At this point Kenneth builds up the agony and heavy breathing until at the
end of the scene one could easily believe that he is in full labour. He wanders
back towards the bench*

Gareth (*holding up the floor of the cot*) Where does this go?
Reg First things first. Where's G? (*He points to one of the sides*) Is that it?

Gareth fetches it and he and Reg attach it to the now almost completed cot

I remember the first cot we ever had. Solid it was. It took three of us to
carry it upstairs. My father made it from an old wardrobe my mother kept
on the landing.

Kenneth is now sitting on the arm of the bench with his back to the audience

Gareth Where is it now?
Reg Gone. We left it in Station Street when we moved to this house.

At this point the bedroom light goes on

You slept many a night in it—it served its purpose.
Gareth I wonder how Shirley is?
Reg She's all right—she's got your mother with her.

Kenneth makes a rather loud noise

What?
Kenneth Eh?
Reg Did you say something?
Kenneth No.
Reg Oh—I thought you said something.
Kenneth (*moving towards them slightly*) Listen. Can I give you a hand?
Gareth (*annoyed*) It's almost finished now. Trust you to offer when it's almost finished.
Reg (*to Gareth*) Come on now, don't start. Pass me the bottom.

Gareth and Reg put the finishing touches to the cot as Kenneth comes round L of the bench and sits on it in the hope of some relief

Gareth I don't know where we're going to put it. Shirley doesn't seem to think it will go by the window.
Reg Well, you'll have to make room for it somewhere.

By now Kenneth's labour is almost at its peak

How's that?

They both stand back to look at it

Gareth (*pleased*) Looks all right, doesn't it?
Reg They don't make them like they used to. Come on, let's take it in.

Reg takes one end and Gareth the other. Gareth is first at the kitchen door stepping backwards into the house. The cot gets wedged in the door frame

It's stuck. Come round a bit.

Gareth manoeuvres the cot to and fro with Reg shouting instructions. After trying for some time without success, even Reg's patience is becoming frayed. The cot is released from the frame

Swap ends.

While tension is building with Reg and Gareth, Kenneth has been contributing more than his fair share, because by now he is almost frantic and as Reg says his last line, Kenneth says his in utter desperation

Now turn it round, turn it round. No towards me, towards me! Not too much! That's right. Now push. (*Shouting*) Push! Push, for God's sake, push!!
Kenneth I am, I am!!

Black-out

Scene 2

The same. About 10 pm the same evening

The Lights come up on Gareth, pacing the lawn in front of the bench. The bedroom light is still on

Reg comes out of the house. He stands in front of the door. He lights his pipe

Gareth (*seeing him*) Anything?

Reg (*shaking his head*) Nothing yet.

Gareth Has the midwife come?

Reg Yes, she's been here about ten minutes.

Gareth Won't be long now then.

Reg (*looking around the garden*) Where's Ken?

Gareth (*sitting on the bench*) I don't know. I think he's gone out. He wasn't looking very good, perhaps he's gone for a walk.

Reg (*sitting next to Gareth*) Why don't you two bury the hatchet, eh?

Gareth What do you mean?

Reg Well, I don't know what's wrong between you, but whatever it is, it's gone on long enough. Even your mother is saying about it.

Gareth What's *she* saying?

Reg How different you are together. Not like brothers at all. You used to get on so well.

Gareth (*getting up and moving down* L) Yeah, well ...

Reg Want to tell your dad about it?

Gareth (*sharply*) No! (*After a slight pause*) Well, there's nothing to tell really.

Reg There must be. There must be something.

Gareth (*shaking his head*) No.   ·

Reg You can't tell me, is that it?

Gareth There's nothing.

Reg I won't be offended if you can't talk to me about it. I just want to help, that's all, if I can.

Gareth (*looking at Reg, smiling and shaking his head*) Thanks, but you can't.

Reg nods, stands and wanders down R *as he re-lights his pipe*

Reg Still no chance of a job, is there?

Gareth No nothing. I thought about joining the army.

Reg Do you think you can do it?

Gareth The money's good.

Reg But do you think you can do it?

Gareth Do you?

Reg (*after a slight pause*) No.

Gareth I don't either.

Reg It's not the place for you.

Gareth moves to the back of the bench and rests his bottom on the back-rest. He is facing away from Reg—back to the audience

Gareth I'm beginning to wonder if there *is* a place for *me*.

Reg Something will turn up. Something will come along, don't worry. It isn't easy I know, especially in the beginning. It's a pity things turned out the way they did.

Gareth looks at him

It's a pity you couldn't have waited a bit longer. You could have saved up a nice little deposit then. Could have bought one of those houses they're building down on the common.

Gareth (*after a slight pause*) Shirley likes those houses. She'd have had one too if I'd been working.

Reg (*after a pause*) I don't want to be nosey - but are things all right with you and Shirley? (*Moving towards the bench*)

Gareth We're as ... how can I put it ... (*moving away from the bench — going more towards the house*) ... we're as well as can be expected.

Reg It *is* difficult I know.

Gareth (*snapping at Reg*) How do you know? How do you know what it's like! We've no privacy—no responsibility—nothing.

Reg I know.

Gareth Everywhere you go there's someone. The only place you can be sure not to bump into anyone is in there. (*He points to the loo*)

Reg It's the same for us, too. We don't have any privacy either. Oh I know it's not the same for me and your mother as it is for you and Shirley, but you can't blame us for that. When we asked you to come and live here all we wanted to do was help you both.

Gareth (*after a pause*) I'm sorry, Dad. I didn't mean to sound ungrateful.

Reg You started off on the wrong foot, that's all. But you're not by yourself. There's thousands like you.

Gareth I don't know so much. (*He pauses. He crosses in front of Reg and goes back to sit on the bench, down* L) I'm in a rut, I know I am and there's nothing I can do about it. I feel so hopeless.

Reg (*joining him*) Is that what it is?

Gareth looks at him

What I mean is, because you haven't got a job? Is that why you've been, well, like you've been.

Gareth (*after a pause*) Yeah.

Reg Then why take it out on Kenneth?

Gareth Do I?

Reg Come on now.

Gareth Well it's not my fault.

Reg Then whose fault is it?

Gareth Ken's. It's Ken's fault. He's a bastard.

Reg He's your brother.

Gareth He's still a bastard.

Reg (*more hurt than angry*) Don't call him that. Don't ever call him that.

Gareth Why not?

Reg I'll tell you why not.

There is a long pause. Reg looks at Gareth then stands. He doesn't find it easy to speak

Back in nineteen fifty ... nine, I think it was, when me and your mother were courting, she had a sister, who died. I don't know if you've heard your mother mention your Auntie Elsie?

Gareth No.

Reg No, well ... she was only nineteen. She left a baby. A lovely little thing he was too. Your mother was working down at Pritchard's at the time. Couldn't afford to throw away jobs in those days either, so your Gran had to rear him. She did her best but she was too old to look after someone so young. (*He pauses*) Me and your mother were getting married the following year anyway, so ... we decided to get married sooner—so we could give the baby a proper home—and a real family.

Gareth So Kenneth's not my brother, then?

Reg He's the same to me and your mother as you are. We've always treated you the same.

Gareth I know. (*A slight pause. He sits on the bench*) He thinks that you and Mam had a shotgun wedding.

Reg (*moving to stand behind Gareth*) Why does he think that?

Gareth He's seen your marriage certificate. He told me a couple of months ago.

Reg (*putting his hand on Gareth's shoulder*) I can't tell you how me and your mother felt when we could see how close you were together. That's what hurts so much to see you now, I suppose. (*After a slight pause*) I don't know what's gone on between you, but perhaps you'll think again now, will you?

Gareth (*after a pause*) Are you going to tell him?

Reg Only when we have to. You won't say anything?

Gareth No.

Reg I'd like him to hear it from us.

Gareth I won't say a word.

Reg Will you tell Shirley?

Gareth Not if you don't want me to.

Reg I'll leave it to you.

There is a pause. Gareth gets up and moves towards the house. He looks up to the bedroom window

Gareth I wonder how she is?

Reg She's a nice girl, Gareth.

Gareth Everyone likes a nice girl.

Reg Hang on to her.

Gareth You reckon?

Reg She'll be all right when she's got a place of her own.

Gareth We don't seem to hit it off very well.

Reg I didn't think I'd settle down with your mother, but I did.

Gareth (*almost to himself*) Yeah, but you had Kenneth keeping you together. (*He pauses*) Dad? Does it make a big difference when the baby's not your own?

Reg You grow to love it in just the same way. Why?
Gareth Nothing. I just wondered, that's all. (*He turns to look at him*)

Doris comes out of the house with a kettle

Doris Oh out here are you?
Gareth Is everything all right?
Doris Yes, it won't be long now. (*To Gareth*) You'd better go up.
Gareth (*amazed*) Me?
Doris Well who else? She's asking for you.
Gareth Upset is she?
Doris No, she's quite calm. I'm surprised at that because I always thought she'd be one of these screaming-for-the-gas-and-air types. But no, she's quite placid. You'd better go up though because she's insisting. I've told her it's not the place for you, but she won't have it. She wants you with her and she won't be put off. Well I can't stop—I've got to take some hot water up.

Suddenly Grandad comes to the kitchen window. He moves the net curtain and hammers on the glass

Grandad Doris, come on for God's sake—bloody standing there gassing—the girl's waiting.
Doris (*to Grandad*) All right I'm coming, I'm coming. (*To Reg*) Look at him ... he's like a dog with two tails. (*To Grandad*) I'll be there now. (*To Gareth*) Don't forget now Gareth—go up—she's waiting.

Grandad hammers on the window even more frantically

All right! All right! (*To Gareth*) Don't be long, it's nearly time.

Doris goes into the house. Grandad disappears from the window

There is a pause. Gareth looks at Reg

Reg Well, go on then.
Gareth What do you suppose she wants?
Reg I don't know. She just wants you there. To hold her hand, I expect.

Gareth looks up at the bedroom window

Gareth We had a row once: and I said then there'll come a time when she'd want me—when she'd call.
Reg (*after a pause*) Go on.

Without turning to face him, Gareth moves towards the house. He is almost at the back door when he stops and turns to face Reg. Reg smiles and nods for him to go

Gareth eventually smiles back and goes into the house

Now Reg is alone. He stands and sighs. He realizes that his pipe has gone out. He takes a box of matches from his pocket and lights up. As he is doing this he strolls around the bench. After he has lit his pipe he shakes the match out and tosses it, as he walks towards the house, into Mrs Morris's garden.

He stops at the kitchen window-sill and checks a begonia plant—then he goes into the house

After a slight pause, the toilet door opens and Kenneth comes out. He looks dehydrated and he is upset. He stands for a moment then looks into the house through the kitchen window. He walks down the garden towards the bench. He is upset and wipes his nose with the back of his hand. As he does this the cries of a new-born baby are heard. He looks up towards the bedroom window

The Lights fade leaving a silhouette of Kenneth in the light from the bedroom window. He runs his fingers through his hair. The light from the window fades leaving the stage in complete darkness

CURTAIN

FURNITURE AND PROPERTY LIST

ACT I

Scene 1

On stage: Path
Small patch of grass
Outside loo
Bucket
Bench
Garden shed
Plants on kitchen window-sill
Fence between gardens
Washing-line in Mrs Morris's garden

Off stage: Part of door handle **(Grandad)**
Basket of washing, pegs **(Mrs Morris)**
Shirt with large burnt hole **(Grandad)**
2 mugs of tea, plaster on cheek **(Reg)**

Personal: **Doris:** wrist-watch, packet of cigarettes, matches in pocket

Scene 2

Strike: Washing from line in Mrs Morris's garden

Off stage: Bottle of gin—required twice **(Grandad)**
Empty bottle of gin **(Grandad)**

ACT II

Scene 1

Set: Deck-chair, newspaper **(for Grandad)**
Shears **(for Reg)**
Washing on line in Mrs Morris's garden

Off stage: Black tie **(Gareth)**
Apple **(Shirley)**
Bottle of aspirin **(Doris)**

Personal: **Kenneth:** comb in pocket
Gareth: blood sac in hand, letter in pocket
Shirley: pregnancy padding
Kenneth: dark glasses

SCENE 2

Strike: Shears, apple core

Set: Box of chocolates, check newspaper **(for Shirley)**

Off stage: Glass of squash **(Shirley)**
Large cardboard box containing enormous toy panda **(Kenneth)**

Personal: **Shirley:** pregnancy padding

ACT III

SCENE 1

Strike: Box of chocolates, newspaper, glass, box, panda

Off stage: Teapot **(Shirley)**
Unassembled cot with instructions in plastic packet **(Reg** and **Gareth)**

Personal: **Grandad:** small bottle of gin, purse with money in pocket
Mrs Morris: money
Shirley: more pregnancy padding
Kenneth: wrist-watch, coin in pocket
Mrs Morris: coin

SCENE 2

Strike: Cot, instructions, etc.

Off stage: Kettle **(Doris)**

Personal: **Reg:** pipe, matches

LIGHTING PLOT

Property fittings required: nil

A garden or back yard. The same scene throughout

ACT I SCENE 1   Morning

To open: Bright morning sunshine

Cue 1   **Doris,** obviously upset, rushes into the house   (Page 14)
            Fade to black-out

ACT I SCENE 2   Evening

To open: General exterior lighting; light in kitchen inside house

Cue 2   **Gareth** slowly turns and walks back into the loo, closing the
            door behind him   (Page 25)
            Fade to black-out

ACT II SCENE 1   Midday

To open: Hot sunny exterior lighting

Cue 3   **Mrs Morris:** "Gareth? Gareth! Gareth."   (Page 41)
            Fade to black-out

ACT II SCENE 2   Afternoon

To open: Sunny exterior lighting

Cue 4   **Gareth:** "... I was a bloody panda."   (Page 49)
            Fade to black-out

ACT III SCENE 1   Evening

To open: Autumn evening lighting; kitchen light on inside house

Cue 5   **Reg:** "... when we moved to this house."   (Page 56)
            Snap on bedroom light inside house

Cue 6   **Kenneth:** "I am, I am!!"   (Page 57)
            Black-out

ACT III SCENE 2   Evening

To open: General exterior evening lighting; bedroom and kitchen lights
           on inside house

Cue 7   Baby cries; **Kenneth** looks up towards bedroom window   (Page 62)
            Fade lights apart from bedroom light

Cue 8   **Kenneth** runs his fingers through his hair   (Page 62)
            Fade light from bedroom window—black-out

EFFECTS PLOT

ACT I

Cue 1   As Scene 1 opens   (Page 1)
Birdsong; radio plays off, inside house

Cue 2   **Doris** (*off*): "... it's half-past nine."   (Page 1)
Increase radio

Cue 3   **Doris** (*off*) "Wake the dead?"   (Page 1)
Decrease radio

Cue 4   **Kenneth** (*off*): "I'm here."   (Page 2)
Plates crash to floor

Cue 5   **Kenneth:** "Get it?"   (Page 5)
Toilet flushes

Cue 6   As Scene 2 opens and throughout scene   (Page 14)
*General party noise from inside house, increasing and decreasing
as back door opens and closes—continue throughout scene; cues
for party noises mentioned specifically in script are given below*

Cue 7   **Gareth** steps out of house and closes door behind him   (Page 14)
Roar of laughter from inside house

Cue 8   **Gareth:** "Yeah, it is stuffy."   (Page 14)
Another roar of laughter from inside, followed by singing

Cue 9   **Gareth:** "... you're having my baby."   (Page 16)
Toilet flushes

Cue 10   **Shirley:** "Oh you are a bastard." They kiss. Back door opens   (Page 24)
Conga music from inside house

Cue 11   All exit into the house, **Kenneth** last, kicking the door closed   (Page 24)
Fade music and party noise

ACT II

Cue 12   As **Gareth** lashes out with his fist   (Page 33)
Sound of glass smashing

ACT III

Cue 13   Shortly after CURTAIN rises on Scene 1   (Page 50)
Toilet flushes

Cue 14   **Shirley** wanders down to bench   (Page 53)
Toilet flushes

Cue 15   **Kenneth** is upset and wipes his nose with the back of his hand   (Page 62)
Cries of a new-born baby

www.ingramcontent.com/pod-product-compliance
Lightning Source LLC
LaVergne TN
LVHW051801080426
835511LV00018B/3376